The
Educator's Guide
to SOLVING
Common
Behavior
Problems

For Katie, Sarah, and Emily, who, on my very best—and their very generous—days, catch a glimpse of who I wish I was.

The
Educator's Guide
to SOLVING
Common
Behavior
Problems

Raymond J. Waller

CORWIN PRESS
A SAGE Company
Thousand Oaks, CA 91320

For information:

Corwin Press	SAGE India Pvt. Ltd.
A SAGE Company	B 1/I 1 Mohan Cooperative
2455 Teller Road	Industrial Area
Thousand Oaks, California 91320	Mathura Road, New Delhi 110 044
www.corwinpress.com	India
SAGE Ltd.	SAGE Asia-Pacific Pte. Ltd.
1 Oliver's Yard	33 Pekin Street #02–01
55 City Road	Far East Square
London EC1Y 1SP	Singapore 048763
United Kingdom	

Printed in the United States of America.

Library of Congress Cataloging-in-Publication Data

Waller, Raymond J.
The educator's guide to solving common behavior problems / Raymond J. Waller.
    p. cm.
Includes bibliographical references and index.
ISBN 978–1–4129–5765–6 (cloth : acid-free paper)
ISBN 978–1–4129–5766–3 (pbk. : acid-free paper)
    1. Problem children—Education—United States. 2. Problem children—Behavior modification. 3. Mentally ill children—Education—United States. 4. Emotional problems of children—United States. 5. Behavior disorders in children—United States. I. Title.

LC4802.W35 2008
371.93—dc22   2007046626

This book is printed on acid-free paper.

08 09 10 11 12 10 9 8 7 6 5 4 3 2 1

Acquisitions Editor:	Jessica Allan
Editorial Assistant:	Joanna Coelho
Production Editor:	Jenn Reese
Copy Editor:	Trey Thoelcke
Typesetter:	C&M Digitals (P) Ltd.
Proofreader:	Andrea Martin
Indexer:	Karen A. McKenzie
Cover Designers:	Monique Hahn, Scott Van Atta
Graphic Designer:	Monique Hahn

Contents

Acknowledgments

I want to offer my sincerest thank you to the graduate candidates who, by taking my classes, continue to teach me more than I teach them; to Dr. Jane McFerrin and Dr. Donna Andrews (my bosses), who have tolerance beyond measure; to Dr. Ray Cleere, who showed grace beyond expectations; and to momma, who did the first editing of this (and my previous) book.

Corwin Press wishes to thank the following peer reviewers for their editorial insight and guidance:

Kimberly Bright
Associate Professor
  of Educational Leadership
  and Special Education
Shippensburg University
Shippensburg, PA

Sally Coghlan
Teacher and Department
  Head
Rio Linda Junior High
Rio Linda, CA

John Hintze
Associate Professor
  and Director of the School
  Psychology Program
University of Massachusetts
  at Amherst
Amherst, MA

Sylvia Rockwell
Behavior Coach
B.T. Washington
  Elementary School
Tampa, FL

About the Author

Photo by
Dr. Bob
Cummings.

Raymond J. Waller is an Associate Professor of Special Education at Piedmont College/Athens and is on the faculty at the University of Georgia in the School of Social Work. He is an active school consultant in the areas of student behavior problems and child and adolescent mental health issues. He has two daughters to whom he frequently pays allowance, three rescued dogs—at least two of which are greatly disliked by his neighbors, and a wife who supervises him during all social gatherings.

1

Introduction

" . . . part of my plan has been to try to pleasantly remind adults of what they once were themselves, and of what they felt and thought and talked, and what queer enterprises they sometimes engaged in."

Mark Twain
Preface to *The Adventures of Tom Sawyer*

I spend a lot of time talking about behavior. Usually I talk about the behavior of other people, since my own behavior is occasionally a source of embarrassment to people, and by "people" I am referring mainly to my spouse. When I was trying to decide what I wanted to do with my life, I found myself continuously leaning toward working with children, for several reasons:

- Kids have fun.
- Kids have candy.
- Kids have toys (see the first bullet point).
- I have a driver's license, so I automatically qualify as "cool," which is a character trait I am unlikely to achieve through merit.
- There really isn't the demand that you would think there would be for lighthouse keepers, despite that misleading song, so I had to scratch that one from my list.

1

One thing that I did not count on when deciding on my career was that adults seem to get really stressed about kids. So even if a kid, let's call him Peanut, since that is the perfect kid name—even if Peanut is thinking that his life is moving along swimmingly, there is almost certainly an adult somewhere that thinks Peanut needs some form of mental health treatment. I think that those of us who are parents *really* want to do what is best for our kids, and those of us that decide to work with kids really want to do good things for kids, *but you'd better* get over the candy idea because they are so not going to share.

So people, as a result of sincere concern, I think, get really serious about children. Often I interact with adults who seem to think every behavioral quirk they see in a child is a sign of deep psychological distress. Sometimes, when I'm listening to adults talking about children, I feel like I'm being blown, page by page, Holden-Caulfield-in-*The-Catcher-in-the-Rye*-style through the process of trying to help a kid, sort of like Pooh kept getting blown, page by windy page, through *The Blustery Day*, with the following major differences:

- Pooh seems to be having more fun than Holden;
- Animals speak with Pooh, and it doesn't surprise Pooh at all; and
- I am, unlike Pooh, wearing trousers.

It's good to be concerned about children and to desire the best for them. I am not certain that you must scowl in order to achieve the best outcome, though. In fact, scowling might be counterproductive. The good news about children and their behavior is that the majority of behavioral issues they develop that are inconsistent with the boundaries adults have deemed appropriate are amenable to change using simple techniques. In fact, you can do these things and never, ever frown. In fact, it probably works better if you don't frown. It will be absolutely unnecessary to wear a facial expression that would communicate to passersby that you are suffering terribly from a painful carpet burn. However, even though the majority of behavioral issues seen in children will respond very favorably to simple techniques that anyone can use effectively, sometimes kids with behavioral problems may require additional help (and this is my serious face). Some of the warning signs that children may need specialized help include:

- A child is unable to effectively function in a setting in which other kids seem to typically function well.
- A child is socially isolated, and either seems uninterested in or incapable of developing relationships with other children of the same age.
- A child has experienced something significantly outside the typical experiences of same-aged peers, such as being maltreated physically or sexually.
- A child is physically and unpredictably violent with peers, despite repeated, clear, age-appropriate attempts to teach expected behavior.
- A child is physically aggressive toward adults, particularly adults usually seen as authority figures, despite repeated, clear, age-appropriate attempts to teach expected behavior.
- A child runs away from supervising adults, despite repeated, clear, age-appropriate attempts to teach expected behavior.
- A child does things that cause pain to animals despite repeated, clear, age-appropriate attempts to teach expected behavior.
- A child shows a high degree of interest in fire.
- A child talks about or engages in intentionally hurting herself or other people.
- A child clearly regresses from some prior level of performance.
- A child engages in actions that compromise her safety or the safety of others, despite repeated, clear, age-appropriate attempts to teach expected behavior.

None of these if observed, is diagnostic. In other words, their occurrence does not tell you that a child has a severe mental health problem. However, these are warning signs that warrant at least getting a professional opinion. When concerns arise, it's also a good idea to consult a physician, because a lot of symptoms that look like they are the result of a mental health issue are actually the result of physical problems that need medical intervention.

Finally, if you are working with a child and you develop concerns that her behavior is really atypical, even if you can't quite put your finger on the nature of your concern, it's best to err on the side of caution. Consult a physician, a psychologist, a social worker, or some other professional with enough expertise in working with children to offer a credible second opinion, and a medical checkup is always a wise precaution.

Having made those stipulations, I can confidently say that the exceptions listed above are *not the most common issues seen in childhood.* Most of the behaviors that children develop that are disruptive, problematic, aggravating, or inconvenient will respond to good behavior support strategies. In fact, even a child who has a diagnosable mental health problem is likely to be helped by the techniques described in this book. So now we can take a deep breath and wipe off the serious face.

This book takes a lighthearted (and hopefully, on occasion, humorous) approach to discussing some of the simple approaches and principles that anyone who interacts with children can use to increase the odds that kids will behave in ways we want. And it is important to wrap your head around that idea—*we can increase the odds of seeing the behaviors we prefer, but there are no guarantees when it comes to human behavior.*

The chapters are short and readable. The strategies therein are based on sound research, and assume that most behavioral issues we see in children result from:

- Skill deficits—things that a child doesn't know or understand, though we might mistakenly assume he *does* understand, and/or
- The undesirable behavior occurs because it *works* for a child in some way or in some setting—even if the behavior doesn't work so well in *our* setting (like a school). So, what this means in a nutshell is that

- Severe mental illness is not usually the culprit, and simple techniques can help in almost all cases.

For those of you who like to "cut to the chase," important points from each chapter are summarized under the heading Points to Remember, listed at the end of each chapter. Suggested readings, for those interested in additional or related study, are also provided at the end of each chapter. With those thoughts in mind, I invite you to consider the issues presented, chuckle on occasion, and either begin the process of understanding children's behavior or pat yourself on the back for already being able to do so.

POINTS TO REMEMBER

- Most behavioral concerns seen in children are responsive to basic management strategies.
- The goal of this book is to help with common behavior management questions and issues.
- I hope this book is occasionally humorous, but never offensive.
- Some students have needs beyond the scope of this book.

The reader who is interested in reading about issues beyond those covered in this book is referred to:

Dogra, N., Parkin, A., Gale, F., & Frake, C. (2002). A multidisciplinary handbook of child and adolescent mental health for frontline professionals. London: Jessica Kingley.

Or to my own personal favorite:

Waller, R. J. (Ed.). (2006). Fostering child and adolescent mental health in the classroom. Thousand Oaks, CA: Sage.

2

Asking the Right Questions

When thinking about the behavior of children, just as when thinking about most other topics, a little bit of knowledge can be dangerous. I can think of a lot of illustrations for this point. For example, I know that health people (not necessarily to be confused with healthy people) say that we should limit our intake of red meat. Health people suggest that we find nutritious substitutes for red meat, such as beans. I know beans are good for me. Even children know that. In fact, often the first piece of prose learned and recited by young boys is a poem that sings the praise of legumes—particularly the positive effects that legumes have on the circulatory system.

But you can image my bean consuming confusion when I gained three pounds after substituting beans for a portion of the red meat that I was regularly consuming. A health person cleared up my confusion by telling me that the gustatory impact of beans does not extend to chocolate-covered espresso beans, which I was consuming by the handful. Who knew?

It's not uncommon for us to become familiar with a new child behavior management strategy (new to us, anyway) and to think that this new strategy (which might also be called a *fad*) is the answer to all of the child behavior questions that we have ever had or may ever have. A couple, friends of mine whose first child was going through the terrible twos, stumbled on a remarkable strategy to solve their child's behavioral challenges—*natural consequences.* Every time their child did something undesirable and experienced an adverse consequence, this couple would join hands and dance merrily ring-around-the-rosies-like as they sang out "natural consequences, natural consequences." It's true that children learn from the consequences of their behaviors (both positive *and* negative), but this does not supplant the need for teaching, parenting, supervision, and intervention. I doubt these parents would sing their natural consequences song as their child played kick the can around the lip of an active volcano.

A more effective approach to behavioral challenges than reliance on the daily miracle strategy is to try to figure out why a challenging behavior is occurring, and a popular approach to finding answers is to ask questions. While asking questions is a good idea, it's probably *not* a good idea to ask a child why he is behaving in an undesirable manner—at least not at first. Initially asking children questions about why they are engaging in an undesirable behavior can lead down a path that is less than productive. Here are just a few of the questions that I have heard teachers ask students *in front of other children:*

"What's wrong with you?"

"Why do you act crazy?"

"Did you take your medicine today?"

I have heard parents ask their children an array of goofy questions, but one of my favorites is the extremely trendy: "Are you ready to clean your room?"

I have found that the best person to start asking questions when a student misbehaves is the teacher, and the question that you should start with is: "Could I do something different that will make this behavior less likely to occur?"

Sometimes people are reluctant to ask this question of themselves because they perceive that the answer assumes or implies *blame*. Let me assure you—asking this question is not about blaming yourself (or anybody else) if a child under your supervision has a behavioral problem. The goal is problem solving, and blame assigning rarely helps with problem solving. The point of asking the question is this: people are different, and people respond to situations in different ways. If there is something that you can do differently, you may be able to prevent the behavior or make it less severe in a very unintrusive way.

The next question that I think can be extremely useful is: "What does the child get out of the problem behavior?"

You really have to be able to step back from the situation in order to answer this question. The answer may seem asinine. A student who steals a pencil from another student does so to get the pencil, right? Maybe. The child could steal a pencil to get your attention. Or to get the attention of other children. Or it could have been a completely impulsive act. Or the child might hate the activity you are about to start and stole the pencil to avoid it by being sent to the office. Looking a little deeper than the first glance can often put you on the path to effective problem solving.

Another question that you should entertain early in your problem solving process is: "Is there a possibility that this is a physical problem?"

I know a man who is a surgical nurse. His five-year-old son started to complain of bellyaches. They tried the over-the-counter remedies and various other things for a few weeks, after which they went to see a pediatrician. The boy was found to have a football-sized abdominal tumor. The story has a happy ending. The tumor was surgically removed and the boy is fine. The father, though, being a nurse, really beat himself up thinking that he should have known that his son had a tumor.

Hindsight, of course, is virtually infallible. The point is that students can have medical issues that cause behavioral symptoms. Though stimulant medications are considered an important component of evidence-based treatment of attention deficit/hyperactivity disorder, failure to administer medicines on a consistent schedule can *result* in behavioral problems. Children can have medical issues such as diabetes that can have behavioral implications. Some medicines used to treat asthma can cause children to go haywire. Two things that continue to surprise me when I'm working with children, and that I always assess if there are behavioral problems, are sleep and caffeine intake. You might be surprised by how many children are in a chronic state of sleep deprivation, which can profoundly affect behavior. Excessive caffeine use, likewise, has become common for many children. I often see young children walking around stores drinking "energy" drinks or latte-type coffee concoctions. If you don't think caffeine can affect your behavior, try going to work without yours.

POINTS TO REMEMBER

- Whenever undesirable behavior occurs, view your approach as "problem solving."
- Avoid the unproductive temptation of blaming—either yourself or the child.
- Try taking a step back, and think about what a child may be getting out of misbehavior.
- Always start by asking what you might do differently—you might find a simple, nonconfrontational solution.
- Children, just like adults, are prone to illness and other physical issues, and some of these can cause or contribute to behavioral problems.

For more discussion, the reader may see:

Chernofsky, B., & Gage, D. (1996). *Change your child's behavior by changing yours: 13 new tricks to get kids to cooperate.* New York: Three Rivers.

3

Just Say "Yo"

As adults, we have a tendency to believe that we can tell someone (particularly a child) what we want him or her to do, or to know, or even to feel, and that, as a result of the wisdom tumbling from our lips, our wishes will be followed. We sometimes tend to think of children as little adults (with runny noses) and we sometimes try to relate to them like we would with each other. However, I have repeatedly found that often, when children are not doing what we want, it is because the child either doesn't understand what we want or doesn't have the foundational skills necessary in order to follow through with our request.

Maybe a few examples will help.

The first problem with giving verbal instructions and assuming that these directions will be followed is that children often misunderstand what they hear. My daughters tend to like the same types of music that I like. I know that they like it because they listen to it. I know I like it because I select it. One of my favorite musicians is Mark Knopfler. One day, they were serenading me with a Mark Knopfler song, *5:15 A.M.*, and should have sung the following line:

La Dolce Vita, 69, all new to people of the Tyne.

My Interpretation: Mark is singing about changes that were occurring, not necessarily positive changes, affecting the Tyne area of England, where he grew up.

However, I heard my children sing:

The Darth Vader's 69, all new at Peeble's for a dime.

My Interpretation: As you might guess, I'm struggling with this one. Undoubtedly, they attempted to place what they were hearing into a frame of reference they could understand.

Lest you be tempted to think that this is simply a misunderstanding stemming from the youth of the listeners, during a car ride, the following line from a Prince song was played on the radio:

Little red Corvette, baby you're much too fast, for my little red Corvette

However, every single adult witness in the car clearly heard my mother-in-law, with enthusiasm, sincerity, and emotion, sing:

Little red Corvette, baby your butt's too fat, for my little red Corvette

The second problem with thinking that simply *telling* people what you want them to do will result in your seeing the desired behavior is that giving verbal directions provides neither the skills nor the motivation to master the task. For example, I can tell you the secret to hitting a major league fast ball. It is extremely simple. I'm going to tell you, and then I want you to do it. All you do is pick up a stick (we baseball fans call this a "bat"), face the person who is about to throw the ball at a high velocity (the "pitcher"), and swing the stick with alacrity as the ball approaches your general position. Simple. If you miss the first time, I may provide the instructions LOUDER, maybe even imply that you lack competence or intelligence. I find that rolling my eyes helps people understand even better than speaking. Surely, these motivators will inspire you to hit the ball on the next try. Since I *taught* you the skills, you must lack motivation. Perhaps laziness is the issue.

You may think that this example is a bit ridiculous, but I don't think so. If you were looking at me, nodding eagerly, and seemed enthusiastic as I told you how to hit a baseball, I might easily assume that you had the elementary skills necessary to meet my expectation. Successful compliance with academic *and* behavioral instructions and expectations are all based on a person's having a previous level of competence and a previous set of skills that *new* skills can be built upon. Often, the children we teach do not have those basics, even if they are cute and smart and eager. In fact, human resources people are now looking for evidence of *behavioral competencies* when they are interviewing and potentially hiring new applicants based on this very issue—people might be able to talk a good game, but the important question is—*do they have the skills necessary to really carry out the job?*

Finally, we have a tendency to think that, if the evidence supports our desired outcome, reasonable people will respond by agreeing with us. We seem almost conditioned to believe that simply *being right* is such a powerful force that it absolutely compels others to join us. If you doubt my proposition, try the following experiment. Go to an established business whose main source of revenue comes from a clientele who travel exclusively by motorcycle. After entering, walk over to any gentleman at the pool table who is either in excess of seven feet tall or 300 pounds and inform him, "My good man, travel by motorcycle is significantly more dangerous than traveling by automobile. You would be an *oaf* to continue to travel by means of a motor driven cycle." Offer to provide references, if you think it will help. And speak with an Australian accent.

The outcome of your intervention on this gentleman's travel habit is unlikely to be of any magnitude beyond his assisting you in getting the most out of your medical insurance. For you number crunchers, that result is not statistically significant. But perhaps the above example is unfair. How about the issue of smoking? Everyone who has ever talked with me about smoking or smoking cessation has said to me that stopping cigarette smoking is the most difficult thing that he or she has ever attempted—*even with* the health warnings on a pack of cigarettes. It isn't that people don't *want* to comply; they simply have been *unable* to comply.

Blah, blah, blah, smoking is bad for you. Tell me *how* to quit. Blah, blah, blah, high school dropouts are almost certainly condemning themselves to poverty. Tell me *how* to be successful in school. Tell me *how* to behave. Tell me *how* to make friends. Then arrange the environment and circumstances so that the odds of my compliance are good. Then show me how. The thing that we have going for us is that kids want to comply. They want to curry our attention and favor. This is an amazingly powerful tool that any of us who works with children can access. Break up any task into small enough pieces for your students to be taught successfully, and teach those skills over and over. Make sure they understand. How many times do you teach them? Until the kids are bored with hearing what you are teaching, until every kid gets it right every time.

The other side of the coin is that this need that children have to get our attention and favor can be used badly. I was recently talking to a support group for parents with children with disabilities. One mother started telling me about how her son's teacher repeatedly made fun of him and belittled him in class. I said, "Bet he doesn't like school."

"He *hates* it," mom said, nodding vigorously.

"If what you're saying is anywhere *close* to being true, I have one thing to say," and I paused. Mom leaned forward expectantly.

"Thank God." Some people in the group actually gasped.

"Why would you say that?" another person in the group asked.

"Because if you put me in a situation where I am constantly degraded in front of my friends, and if I know that nothing

I do will measure up, and I know that I will have to face this day after day after day, I would hate it too. So would you. If your kid *liked* that, I would really be worried about him."

Points to Remember

- Expect children to *not* understand what you want or expect until they *show* you that they do understand.
- When you have the goal of teaching a new skill, break it up into small tasks and teach each task.
- Teach students your expectations clearly and repeatedly.
- Reteach your expectations until all of your students meet the expectations *all of the time.*
- Set up the environment to maximize the odds for success and model your expectations.
- Continue to teach your expectations occasionally.

The interested reader who wants to know more about behavioral competencies in hiring practices:

Should consult someone with a much better track record than I have at maintaining employment.

The reader who is interested in cutting edge knowledge (and lack of knowledge) relating to smoking cessation may refer to:

National Institutes of Health. (2006). NIH state-of-the-science conference on tobacco use: Prevention, cessation, and control. *NIH Consensus and State-of-the-Science Statements, 23*(3). Retrieved October 2, 2007, from http://consensus.nih.gov/2006/TobaccoStatementFinal090506.pdf

4

Have a Plan

"Hope for the best but plan for the worst." I don't know who originally said that, but it applies to any person who works with children. Plan for everything you can think of, and then make a contingency plan so that, when the stuff that you didn't think about occurs, you have a plan to put into place. And it will happen (whatever *it* is). Peanut will come to school in a snit, and it will happen. And you will remain cool and confident in the face of the unknown, because you have a plan, and you *never*, ever want to look dazed or confused.

That is not to suggest in any fashion that you don't ever appear to make a mistake. I think that it is absolutely *vital* for you to make mistakes. Otherwise, the example that you are setting is beyond the reach of us mere mortals. You should make some mistakes (don't go wild with it or anything), you should acknowledge your mistakes, and you should correct your mistakes. If the mistake involved another person— particularly a student—apologize sincerely. The children around you need to see your mistake and they need to see a good model of how mistakes are handled.

Looking unprepared, shocked, or discombobulated is a different ballgame. Your nonverbal language needs to absolutely shout "I'm in charge and I'M NONPLUSSED!" I assure you, you will never be able to plan for every possibility, so don't even try. Just have a plan for the unexpected. I provide the following (true) example, not to be edgy but to show that you can never plan for everything that can happen around a group of students.

When starting a recent year in the classroom as a teacher, I was pretty sure I had behavior right where I wanted it. I was teaching a self-contained class of fourth- to sixth-grade boys labeled as having emotional/behavior disorders. Every one of the boys had a background of fighting, so I was really focused on preventing physical confrontations. The Christmas break was approaching, and not one fight had occurred. I was strutting around the classroom one day, trying not to rub calluses on my hand by patting myself on the back for my noteworthy behavior management prowess, when it happened.

All of a sudden, it was like the fire alarm sounded. My senses went on high alert and glands in my body began to madly pump adrenalin throughout my body, priming my central nervous system to fight or flee. The alarm reaction began to localize itself to my olfactory nerves. If I had been holding two small melon scoops, I would have surgically removed my own nasal passages. As I watched, the other students registered the stench. Some broke low and others broke high in desperate but fruitless attempts to escape. All of this happened in milliseconds, along with the realization that this attack to our noses had *come from inside* of one of my students. My classroom was equipped with a back door that opened to a vacant lot behind the school, and we all simultaneously made for that door. Had anybody been outside, our egress would have looked, if turned upward, like somebody had kicked over a fire ant bed. And through all of this, my nearly fatal mistake was that I was, in fact, dazed and confused by this unforeseen turn of events.

Thus began perhaps the worst week of my life. The boys saw weakness and they exploited that weakness. I don't blame them—it's what kids do. It's their job. But my job had become more treacherous than I had expected. That incident began the most horrible period of systematic torture I ever endured. Our school days became syncopated by mad escapes from the stench drenched torments. Each time it happened we resembled a bunch of circus clowns leaving a small circus clown car, except we didn't wear floppy shoes, and what an onlooker may have originally thought were painted on smiles were actually genuine grimaces. Occurring throughout the true emergencies were "false alarms," and we were all so conditioned by the abuse that any sudden movement, no matter how slight, by anyone toward the back door resulted in a veritable explosion of desperate flight to atmospheric freedom.

Not much teaching occurred during that week. Around Thursday evening, I realized that I hadn't followed my own guidelines. My *super contingency after unforeseen contingencies plan* was "If all else fails, punt." Or as I like to call it, Mr. Spock's Treatise—"When all else fails, when logic is inconclusive and when data are inconclusive, trust a hunch." Friday morning after the bell rang and when everybody was seated, I opened the back door and placed a plastic chair about three feet *outside* the classroom. I had their attention now. I said, "Guys, we haven't been able to get much done this week because of all of the whizpopping." (Some of you may recognize the term *whizpopping* from *The BFG* by Roald Dahl—a book I had read recently aloud to the class.) My statement was met with nods, murmurs of agreement, and yes, some sly smirks.

"Starting today, no more running from the room. If anybody needs to whizpop, you're free to go sit in this chair to do it. In fact, if you need a break for any reason, feel free to enjoy the sunshine." I was all smiles.

Then my look became serious.

"But if anybody has any 'accidents' in the classroom, which I am labeling TODAY as a no whizpop zone, *I'm* taking an outside break. You guys need to just keep doing your work, and you can have your turn at having a break after I have mine."

I pointed around the room to the NO WHIZPOPPING signs I had posted. And then I smiled again, an evil Grinchy smile like I had just schemed to steal Christmas from the Whos. And in a way I had.

The boys looked at me. One ventured cautiously, "You wouldn't do that to us, would you doc?" No words, just a smile in response. Another boy said completely without emotion, "Oh, yeah, he'll do it."

A three second pause ensued, after which some magical divination apparently occurred whereby every boy in the classroom immediately knew who in the class had apparently been subsisting on rotten meat and sour milk for the past week. Peer pressure was a wonderful thing to watch, and I never had to follow through on my threat. And none of the boys in the class got into a fight that year, either.

POINTS TO REMEMBER

- It is the job of children to try to find ways to circumvent your rules. That is more fun than math worksheets.
- Things will happen when you work with children that you *never dreamed* would happen.
- Develop at least two plans to address "emergencies" that *could* occur in your class. Examples of potential emergencies include:
  - A child wets her pants in class.
  - A fight breaks out.
  - You give a child a direction and he looks at you and refuses.
  - A medical emergency (such as a severe asthma attack) arises.

The reader who is interested in more of Mr. Spock's logic and proverbs should swing by the house—I have every Star Trek *paperback in print up through about four years ago, when I just ran out of time for it.*

Any reader interested in the intricacies of whizpopping is referred to the excellent:

Dahl, R. (1982). *The BFG*. Middlesex, UK: Penguin.

And for anybody with more curiosity than that, I can only offer the following referral:

Domis, M. W. (2004). *Thoughts from the commode*. White Plains, NY: Peter Pauper.

The Importance
of Bonding

After I was married, one of the things that my wife thought would be a great "couples activity" for us was shopping, an activity that involved the two of us going to various places from which consumer goods could be purchased for one of us. We developed a "couples ritual," in which she would suggest that we go to a store, I would bellow, trying my best to sound like a birthing walrus, and she would ignore me, and then we would go to the store of her choice. One day, she suggested that we go shopping for new shoes, and I burst forth in walrus song—and here's the funny part: she thought I was being funny. In fact, I was trying to communicate my pain.

Nonetheless, we went shopping. We went to numerous shoe stores—probably hundreds (I lost track after a while)—and eventually I found myself sitting on one of the little shoe benches, trying to find my imaginary happy place, and waiting. In fact, I did find my imaginary happy place, and my happy place apparently included a large population of ducks. I honestly don't know how it happened, but I found myself making duck sounds, not just in my happy place *but right there in the shoe store* and not just in my imagination but *with my real-life mouth.* In fact, I was "in the zone" as far as duck communication goes. I was the veritable Shakespeare of duck speak, quacking with articulation and passion. The problem arose because I had apparently entered the zone with duck talk at precisely the same moment that my wife placed a newly shoed foot in front of me and asked my opinion. I maintain to this day that her asking my opinion about the aesthetic appeal of her shoe and my becoming the living voice of duck speak was completely unrelated—that they were simply the kind of unfortunate coincidences that resulted in things like the sinking of the *Titanic.*

I learned some very important things that day. The first was that ducks are often associated with big feet. The second was that, though most of my friends cared even less about the prospect of my suggesting that they have big feet than, say, my telling them that the sky is blue, *some people are mortified and offended to the very core of their being* if some thought, behavior, or action suggests that *they* have big feet. I left "the zone" of duck speak and my happy place, slowly becoming aware that I was not the only person who had entered "the zone." My wife had entered a zone of absolute perfection as it relates to giving me "the look." She was so deeply in the zone that her right eye was actually twitching.

In your relationships with other people, you have ways of communicating your feelings to those about whom you care. Perhaps, just perhaps, you either give or receive "the look." If your life resembles mine, the look communicates disapproval. In the situation described above, the look resulted in my understanding that I had done something bad and the behavioral outcome was immediate silence on my part. The reason that the look had this effect is because my wife and I have a relationship, and as a result of that relationship, I actually care if she gives me "the look." If *you* were to disapprove of some animal sound I was making, and if you gave me the look in a shoe store, it's unlikely that I would give it more thought than to maybe briefly consider that the look on your face was trying to tell me that you had consumed a spoiled seafood product.

When I was working on a bachelor's degree in special education, I vividly remember what a previous mentor said in a class about behavior management: "When you enter your class for the first time, find a kid who is breaking a rule, and make an example out of him." While I learned some very useful things from this person, the above advice was not one of them. The advice is really bad in many ways and on numerous levels. But here is one of the most basic flaws with the advice: no matter what kind of behavior management plan you use, the effectiveness of your plan will be dramatically improved if you have bonded (or have a positive relationship) with your students.

Sometimes when I say that the overall effectiveness of your behavior management plan is dependent on having a positive relationship with your students, some teachers will misinterpret the advice to bond with their students and to assume that this means that you must be their "buddy." This is *not* the point. In fact, trying to be your student's buddy is almost certain to have a bad outcome. Someone's feelings will get hurt, someone will be let down, or you will be taken advantage of or become a joke among (at least some of) your students.

Bonding with your students does involve those skills that help promote positive relationships in other areas of your life. Skills that build positive relationships with children are the same as the skills associated with building relationships with adults. Those skills involve such behaviors as listening to others, giving the benefit of the doubt, assuming the best (rather than the worst) about your students, letting your students have a voice in what happens in the classroom, and taking responsibility to try to accommodate their interests.

Consider some of the advantages of bonding with your students. Children have a developmental need for nurturing from adults, so you will be meeting one of their most important desires and fundamental necessities. Bonding with your students facilitates a positive learning environment. Bonding with your students is much more likely to establish school as a safe and good place to be than your making a bad example out of them. Bonding in fact is much better for *you*, because a negative, coercive environment has well-established undesirable outcomes *even for those in charge*. Having a positive relationship with your students also provides protection for you, in that it's a "buffer" for those times that you make mistakes or you're not at your best—and we all have those times. Finally, if you have a positive relationship with your students, you can sometimes use minimal interventions such as "the look," whereas if your students don't think you really care about them or if they feel antagonistic toward you, the minimal disapproval communicated by the look is irrelevant. One caveat about strategies like "the look"—if you use them too frequently, they will lose their effectiveness. That's a point we are still working on at home . . .

POINTS TO REMEMBER

- Never, *ever* make a bad example out of a student. Even if it communicates terror to the others, you have probably lost your opportunity with the one you made an example out of forever. In addition, the others will, rightfully, distrust you.
- There is no down side to bonding with your students.
- Bonding with your students not only promotes student investment in the school environment, it promotes the students' looking after you while you look after them.
- Bonding involves those basic skills that result in your developing positive relationships in other areas of life. It *does not* involve being a "buddy."

Readers who find themselves in the pickle I was in at the shoe store may want to plead their case using the example of:

Seuss, D. (1965). *I wish that I had duck feet*. New York: Random House.

6

If You Don't Beat Them, They Will Never Learn

A few weeks ago, my wife and I and another couple were invited to eat at the home of a coworker of mine. Since we are extremely selective about whom we allow to watch our children and nobody was available except my relatives, we took our two daughters with us. After we had visited a while, one of my coworkers said, "My goodness, your daughters are wonderful! How do you manage to have such well-behaved girls?"

"I threatened them on the way over here," I answered.

Ha ha ha, my coworkers chuckled heartily, as my children and I watched them and my wife looked at the floor.

"Really, I threatened them," I assured, wanting to impress my friends with my behavioral prowess.

"Yeah, he did," both of my offspring deadpanned. The chuckling, along with the conversation, withered and died. I haven't been invited back.

I never seem to be able to reconcile our societal obsession with punishment. We absolutely quiver with glee at the opportunity to "give somebody what they deserve." After all, "all they need is a good beating," right? From smackdowns to Texas Rangers to Court TV to corporal punishment, we know that the world will be right if we can impose some much needed whooping on some deserving slob. Of course, where I grew up, a "good beating" was one that somebody else received.

Rather than focus on pie-in-the-sky "moralizing" about things like forgiveness, nurturing, teaching, and compassion, it might be wise to present some of the known side effects of punishment for discussion purposes. Before proceeding, it should be acknowledged that not *every person* who receives punishment will experience side effects. In fact, all of us are punished sometimes. For example, getting turned down when asking somebody on a date is a punisher for many people (uh, you got turned down, too, didn't you?). In fact, some people might receive a lot of punishment and "do okay." The question that you need to ask yourself is, "How am I going to play the odds?"

If you're comfortable with knowing that there is a *good chance* that you will cause more harm than good if you expose children to harsh or physical punishment, then it's fine to base your behavior management plan on the use of punishment. It's hardly in dispute by any child and adolescent mental health professional that harsh punishment can cause harm in a variety of ways. If the odds are worth it, though, play them. Wait—if the odds are acceptable *for your own child,* go for it. Your child, no doubt, needs a good beating once in a while. Don't let it bother you that punishment (particularly physical punishment) is about as likely to result in aggression from the punishee as it is to reduce an undesirable behavior. Your kid can take it. Don't get bogged down by how easy it can be to turn a child against learning and schools, and don't stress yourself with the knowledge that it's pretty hard to get a child reinvested in school after that child has gotten turned off.

If you're comfortable acknowledging that punishment is, by nature, associated with such mental states as anxiety and depression, then batter up. Don't preoccupy yourself with the problem that these mental states are *completely contrary to the learning process.* Punishment is like vitamin C—without the necessary amount, kids just don't function well. Don't put yourself in a dither just because the vast majority of documented cases of child maltreatment start off as "punishment" and then go too far. Vegas is not the clearinghouse sweepstakes— you are not guaranteed to win. You pays your nickel and you takes your chances.

Don't stress over the problem of we humans being adaptable. In fact, we can adapt to virtually any aversive situation or stimulus. If you start off yelling to get compliance with a three-year-old, it won't be long before yelling becomes less effective. Then you have to go to the next level. But what will you have left when the child is eight? Don't worry that punishment doesn't teach a new skill. In the *best* of circumstances, it teaches what you don't want. But, in the absence of teaching replacement skills, relapse of the punished behavior can be high. And don't fret that kids that you think you're punishing are actually playing you a lot of the time—don't hate the player, hate the game.

I know that it will surprise you, but, during my high school years, I was a frequent recipient of corporal punishment at school. Often partaken several times a week. Always strategically administered during nonpreferred activities, as defined by (1) algebra or (2) chemistry. "Old three-licks-or-three-days Waller" they called me—retired my boxers when I graduated. Frankly, the whole thing was embarrassing—and by that I mean I was embarrassed for the assistant principal. He would sigh deeply when I walked into the office. "Armpit music again, Waller?" (I believe the word *prodigy* applied to me on this, my virtuoso instrument.) "Three licks or three days?"

"Licks," I would grunt, looking down at the perspiring administrator. If you completely ignore themes of intelligence and character, I was twice the human that the assistant principal was in terms of biological mass. He knew and I knew that I could, at my whim, place my right hand on the top of his head and press downward, compressing him until there was nothing visible but his prominent administrator forehead and big floppy shoes plopping him around the hall like one of those squatty robot vacuum cleaners, randomly demanding to see your hall pass.

That didn't happen, of course. He played the game, and I played the game, and here I am. He didn't "punish" my behavior, in the sense that he presented something to reduce a target behavior. Just like my "threat" to my own children really had no impact on their behavior at the dinner with coworkers. On the way to my coworker's home, we told them what our expectations were. We covered possibilities that might arise and how we would handle them. We may have even mentioned to them that their own preferred activities for the rest of the weekend could be impacted if their behavior didn't adhere to the rules that we knew that they knew that we knew (if you can follow that). They were sweating bullets.

POINTS TO REMEMBER

- If you didn't catch it, most of this chapter was written using a literary style known as *sarcasm*.
- Many, many people support the use of corporal punishment and other types of punishment-based approaches to behavior management.
- Whatever your opinion of punishment as an approach to behavior management, you need to be aware that the evidence is overwhelming: punishment carries the risk of numerous, undesirable side effects.
- Punishment is more likely to turn a child off of learning and school than to excite them about learning and school.
- It's a lot harder to get children interested in school once they have formed a negative view of it than it is to turn children off of learning and school.
- If you have a good relationship with your students, very mild punishers such as "the look" (reread the previous chapter if you already forgot) will probably get the job done.

Any reader interested in the topic of corporal punishment absolutely should not miss reading:

Hyman, I. A. (1997). *The case against spanking: How to discipline your child without hitting.* San Francisco, CA: Jossey-Bass.

7

Meeting Developmental Needs

P eople decide to work with young children for a variety of reasons. Kids are cute, in a runny-nosed sort of way. They are faithful. Let's face it, a sizable percentage of them think that a large beneficent hare frolics around the globe one day each year, hiding eggs willy-nilly for the sole purpose of amusing these believing children. Two things, kids:

1. Mammals don't lay eggs!
2. If the rabbit wanted you to have the eggs, he wouldn't hide them!

Another great thing about children is that they think that we are smart—at least until they reach their thirteenth birthday—even if we haven't picked up a book since reading about that boy who ran, ran, ran around chasing a girl he had a thing for named Jane. Or am I thinking of Tarzan? It doesn't matter, because children will believe you. Their main source of information is otherwise-unemployable people in character costumes, while *we* have the added educational advantages of a later bedtime *and* prime time animated television. And children depend on us for *everything.* It's a humbling responsibility to consider, outweighing that aggravation that their needs, inconsiderately, don't always schedule themselves to occur during commercial breaks.

If you decide to have children, or if you decide to work with children, you make a huge commitment. Either of these endeavors is a lifestyle choice, and affects many of the subsequent decisions you can make about your life. In fact, when you really think about it and consider the costs involved in making the commitment that we must make to children, the pleasure derived from watching cute runny noses isn't much payback. It seems like they would appreciate us, in words, thoughts, deeds, perhaps even in song.

And now for a deep, cleansing breath. Children depend on us to meet all of their needs. In some manner—choice, desire, or behavior—you have decided that you want to participate in helping to meet their needs. If you are now or if you aspire to become a teacher, some of your students may come in and greet you with smiles and sonnets every day. They may give you presents and make you cards. Some of them may hold you in such high esteem that it's incredible that a spirit as omnipotent as yours actually fits into an earthly vessel.

But you can rest assured that *not all* of them will respond to you like this. In fact, our society doesn't really seem to value the level of commitment that you are making to its children (who are our future, I am told). It is the job of any of us who decide to invest ourselves in the lives of children to *meet their needs* while we engage in the process of teaching them to *meet their own needs.* You, by virtue of having attained your eighteenth birthday, have been credentialed by society as being capable of meeting your own needs. You are on the wrong track if you want or expect children to meet *your* needs. However, a highly trained mental health professional may be able to help. Come see me. I'll give you a discount—I like you.

Years ago, I worked in juvenile justice. One of the things that my boss used to tell kids who had gotten caught breaking the law was, "90 percent of the kids who break the law don't get caught. You're obviously not good at breaking the law, so you need to stop." (Man, I had some great mentors.) Despite my doubts about the 90 percent figure (and my doubts about the wisdom of the advice that went with it), there are some important things for you to keep in mind. Most kids *will*, in fact, break the law before they reach the age of eighteen, and most of the law breakers will not get caught. Fortunately, most of the laws broken are not going to be serious felony-type crimes. Many of them will be *status offenses*—things illegal for children but not for adults (like not adhering to curfews or not following caregiver instructions).

All children are going to break the rules sometimes. In some ways, it is a kid's job to figure out ways to get around the rules. A natural outcome of seeking out their boundaries is that they will step over them once in a while. It will prepare them for later life tasks, like coming up with plausible excuses to call in sick. However, as my former boss said, some children are better at breaking the rules without getting caught than others. At the risk of my repeating some of the material already discussed in previous chapters, keep this in mind: if you focus on punishing behaviors you don't like, *some children will be treated unfairly.* The final result is that the children who are the *least skilled* at breaking the rules will be punished disproportionately—they will get most of the punishment even though they won't necessarily be breaking the most rules. They just get caught more because they're not as good at it. The cute, smiling, *sneaky* ones are breaking rules, too, at all odds. They are just better at it— so they basically are *rewarded* for breaking rules. But they are also more likely to meet our needs by being adoring of us—or engaging in those things that have sometimes been called *teacher pleasing behaviors.*

Another point that is important to consider is that the students who don't engage in a lot of teacher pleasing behaviors may, in fact, need you much more than the students who adore (or are good at pretending that they adore) you. Following one of the primary themes of this book—children who don't actively endear themselves to you may lack the *skills* to do so, rather than lack the *desire* to do so. In cases where skill deficits exist, it's necessary to teach the skills. And keep in mind that children who are challenging—because they are overly active, they have a difficult temperament, or they don't engage in adult pleasing behaviors—are much less likely than other children to foster positive interaction, especially with adults. So the students who are not pleasing you may *need* you very badly, although for a variety of potential reasons (including a lack of knowing how to obtain your positive attention) they seem on the surface to thwart your efforts at bonding.

All of this fits into a broader context involving how students perform in relation to *how we expect them to perform.* If we expect them to get in trouble, we tend to catch them breaking the rules. If they are our favorites, we tend to catch them doing our favorite things. Our expectations have a strong influence on what we perceive—and they influence how other people act. I wonder if we, those who choose teaching as our mission, shouldn't follow a practice of physicians. Physicians subscribe to the Hippocratic Oath as a conceptual roadmap that is supposed to guide their professional practice. The Hippocratic Oath is the statement of personal conduct from which the concept of "first do no harm" is cited (which is ironic since the Hippocratic Oath does not contain those words). We should take an oath acknowledging that teaching is a human service, that we have high expectations for all students, that we will pursue every possibility of ensuring success for every child, things like that. But *not* the Hippocratic Oath—unless you pray to the god Apollo.

Finally, you need to brace yourself for the inconceivable eventuality that a student, at some point in your career, may really just *not like you,* despite how wonderful your mother told you that you are. It is a hurtful thing to not be liked, especially when we have given a relationship our best efforts.

Before you let yourself wallow in despair, though, think about all of the people that you have worked with or known in your life. Has there ever been anybody that you have known that tried to be nice to you but, for some reason—even if you couldn't *actually put your finger on the reason*—no matter what they did *you just didn't like them that much*? My guess is that the answer is yes. Perhaps you are now in a domestic partnership with that person. Sometimes our personalities just clash. But it isn't reasonable—nor is it necessary—to make such a clash personal. We like different types of music. If you don't like the same type of music that I do, it doesn't make one of us worse. We like different things. Even when it comes to people, we have different tastes; just don't forget who is responsible for meeting the developmental needs of whom. But at the end of the day, you can still call momma.

POINTS TO REMEMBER

- All children need positive adult attention—it's a developmental need as important as food.
- Some children may not have the necessary skills to engage in teacher pleasing, but those skills can be taught.
- Just because children seem to try *really hard* to show you that they don't care if you like them, they probably want you to like them.
- There may be the occasional student who *really doesn't* like you, just because your personalities clash. It's as unreasonable to hold this against a child as it would be to hold against a child that she has a different taste in music.
- Don't forget (this bears repeating): it's your job to meet the child's needs, not vice versa.

The interested reader who wants to see the Hippocratic Oath in its entirety can do so at:

http://www.indiana.edu/~ancmed/oath.htm

Any reader interested in the relationship between one's own needs and one's chosen vocation may want to peruse:

Naylor, T. H., Willimon, W. H., & Osterberg, R. (1996). *The search for meaning in the workplace.* Nashville, TN: Abingdon.

8

Move Those Buns!

I don't know about you, but when I was in school, we had the opportunity on *a daily basis* to go outside and move around for a while in relatively unstructured play time. By relatively unstructured I mean that one day in elementary school two friends and I left the playground, entered some nearby woods, found several junk tires, took them (and ourselves) back to the playground to the top of a large hill, and took turns folding ourselves into these junk tires and rolling each other down the hill. Once at the bottom, we came to a stop with the assistance of a convenient tree or classmate, then it was back up the hill to do it all again. We started this activity before Christmas, and (remember, the point was "unstructured" time) played this game for the rest of the school year.

Even in high school, there were two scheduled daily breaks—one in the morning and another in the afternoon. Although there was no playground, we still mingled about and socialized—and (at least some people) smoked. Yep, in my day principals, apparently understanding the volatile dynamic that can occur over the synergistic effects of saturation of hormones and an adolescent having a nicotine fit, took the high road. Oral tobacco products were quite popular where I went to school, but it's only fair to tell you (and I am not making this up) that the annual steer show was an excused absence from school (and I went every year). While I never used *any* tobacco product, this did not prevent my figuring out very quickly how much movement and excitement one could inspire by placing a piece of chocolate between teeth and gums, allowing it to melt, and expectorating in close proximity to other adolescents.

Today, schools don't offer nearly as many opportunities for students to *move.* We seem to find it desirable for children to sit still and be quiet, do and enjoy school work, walk *quietly* down the hall *in a straight line*—some schools don't even allow students to talk during lunch. One day at lunch when I was a senior in high school I sang a contemporary country music hit, word for word, to a mortified school administrator (and the other massed diners), and some kids in schools today *aren't allowed to talk* during lunch!

I promise you that such expectations are not realistic, they're not healthy, and they *contribute to* the occurrence of behavior problems in school. Some teachers apparently think that allowing—even encouraging—students to move around is counterproductive. If the tight reins of structure are ever slackened, these teachers seem to think, the students will respond to some primal urge to do terrible things to school property involving melted chocolate morsels and saliva.

So my interest was particularly piqued when my youngest daughter, who was then in the third grade, began dropping snippets and hints about some of the things that her teacher did. I heard words like *music, jumping, dancing.* Actually, I heard even more things that convinced me, with a fair degree of certainty, that her teacher was a nut. Intrigued, I asked this teacher if I could come observe. Completely nonplussed, she consented. I don't know how to describe her (besides the aforementioned "nut")—maybe some hybrid genetic cross between Mary Poppins and Roger Rabbit. But *all* of the kids paid attention to her. They all participated. They even smiled.

Rather than try and fail to describe what this teacher—in my opinion the best intuitive manager of child behavior I ever observed—did, I asked her to do so. She graciously consented to share some of her strategies below.

Keep Them Hopping

Michael Rice Miller

I have found that "motivation" is the main variable that students face. Many of our traditional teaching methods depend on the child's "inner motivation" and often teachers can "lose" students due to constantly assigning overly structured and controlling tasks. Many of the behavior problems that appear in classrooms today occur because the students become bored just sitting. I feel that when there is more movement and music within a classroom setting, all learners will become motivated and excited about the learning process. An added element to this equation is relating the classroom material and motivational strategies to the lives of all learners.

Most of our traditional classrooms today are set up according to an almost cookbook approach—sit down, read, write—and we are seeing more behavior problems and moments of distress because of these practices. Teaching in a K–5 setting today is not like it was in years gone by. Most regular education teachers today have the daunting task of teaching students with special needs (daunting because regular ed. teachers have little knowledge of how to work with students with disabilities), gifted students, students with severe academic challenges, students whose first language is not English, and students who have experienced tragedies within their own homes.

Getting Started

Before I begin a lesson, I make sure that all my learners are mentally prepared. We often do simple exercises that involve various musical selections. Before writing, a favorite music activity of my students is to push their palms in the air and rotate their hands in a circular motion. I have found this to be a good strategy to "clean the slate," let the children listen to music and move, and to get my learners excited and ready for the next task. Some of the other things that my students love the most include:

The Stomp—All students' favorite. Begin slowly stomping your foot and clapping this pattern: "Stomp, stomp, clap; stomp, clap; stomp, stomp, clap" as you chant, "We think we are special." Then I insert each child's name in the chant: "We think _____ is special."

My Favorite Attention Grabbers!

Wear silly glasses—I purchase some extra large clown glasses at the local dollar store.

Blow bubbles—I love to wear my bubble necklace and blow bubbles to mark that I need all eyes on me.

Make music—Play a certain song that students know and teach them that this is a signal to stop what they are doing and focus their attention on me. Play a music box (I purchased a Cinderella music box at my local department store), ring a bell, and so on.

Put on a hat—I have various hats that I wear for different occasions and that I use as different signals.

POINTS TO REMEMBER

- Come up with ways to *let them move!*
- It's okay to have fun.
- Teach your students when a lot of movement is okay, and teach them when you want them to be in their seats.
- The best way to deal with behavior problems is to *prevent them* by meeting the needs of your students, not to *cause them* by trying to be too strict, structured, or controlling.
- You can use your own signals and attention grabbers to convey messages. Not only are they fun, they will help you avoid the temptation of raising your voice to manage behavior.
- I didn't mention it, but this "nut" who shared some of her ideas with us was "teacher of the year" when my daughter was in her class.

Readers interested in taking the plunge and trying some of the types of activities that Michael is talking about should check out one of her favorite Web sites:

http://www.enchantedlearning.com

The Anxiety
Trap

Something that truly shocked me about being a college professor who currently teaches only graduate candidates is how vehement my graduate students are about *not wanting to be* assessed by taking tests. I have often found, of course, that the people that whine the loudest about *taking* tests— usually citing "test anxiety" as the problem with their personal test taking (in)ability—are typically the ones most likely to *give* tests to their own students. As a highly trained mental health professional, my response is that I am sympathetic to the negative effect that anxiety can have on learning and on communicating what you have learned. As a person who thinks that it is unreasonable to expect more out of children *than you expect from yourself,* my response is WOO WOOOO! I hate a hypocrite!

Anxiety problems affect more people than any other mental health issue. They can be as focused as the person with a catastrophic fear of snakes or as diffuse as the person who is unable to go out in public because of the overwhelming anxiety that leaving their home inspires. Well-meaning people who see these anxiety responses in friends or family sometimes attempt to offer assistance by assuring the anxious people that their fear and apprehension are unreasonable compared with actual level of danger. Though well-meaning, this is, at least on some level, insulting—people often know that their anxiety is unreasonable. However, you are about as likely of talking people out of blinking when a light is shined in their eyes as you are of talking people out of their anxiety.

Anxiety does not affect only adults. Children experience anxiety—and can have anxiety disorders—just as can adults. In children, one source of overwhelming anxiety for too many students is school. Think about it—children, at a very young age, are taken to a place that they have never been before. Some of them have never had substantial separation time from parents or caregivers. Some have heard bad stories about school from siblings and other kids. Many have never been alone in such a large group of totally new faces. And some of them are picking up on the anxiety that their parents feel as they are left at school. This is not exactly the recipe for nap time.

To make matters worse, it seems that anxiety is a strategy that we sometimes fall back on to change the behavior of others when we don't know what else to do. Does "just wait till your father gets home" ring a bell? Anxiety causes suffering and avoidance. Of course, suffering and avoidance are not mental states that promote *learning,* so it doesn't seem wise that we would use anxiety as a behavioral strategy in the schools. We also (and I hate to say it) resort to *lying* in order to maximize the anxiety effect, and kids will pick up on it pronto if you are lying to them—even if you aren't intentionally lying. For years, we (and by we I mean you, not me) told kids that smoking pot would basically kill them. Some kids, being kids, invariably went out and experimented with pot and then afterward wasted little time telling every person they saw that they were in fact alive.

We tell some other whoppers in school—at least in my opinion—and we seem to do this under the mistaken assumption that students will *learn better* if we can cause them to be *anxious enough.* We tell kids in high school that we have to pound content into them if they want to make it in college. We teach them algebra, and if they don't develop some nervous condition during a year of algebra we put them in geometry, and if they are foolish enough to come back when they are seniors we cram them into trigonometry. "You'll need this for college" we tell them. And they go off to college and most of them are only required to take one math class *and it's algebra,* and they haven't practiced algebra for three years. So a lot of them don't do so well, and a lot of those who don't do so well quit college because they think they are dumb, when the *real* problem is that we lied to them and they haven't practiced algebra for three years. Same with English 101, except we shove them into advanced literature courses, and they fail English 101 because they don't remember what a gerund is. And they end sentences with prepositions.

So then we give them tests that we say will kill them if they don't pass, practice "intruder" drills, and implement zero-tolerance policies. More than ten years' worth of research suggests that zero-tolerance policies, by the way, can actually increase (rather than decrease) behavior problems—and encourage kids to drop out of school. Teachers aren't left out of the anxiety trap either—more students, less planning time, demands for inclusion without adequate resources to make it work, and being held "accountable" based on measures that don't really appraise job competence are a few common (and valid) complaints. But right now we are talking about the students. We cannot relate to people with whom we have lost credibility. We cannot bond with kids while trying to scare them. We cannot manage the behavior of students who dislike us. And we cannot teach students who will not allow us to influence their behavior.

POINTS TO REMEMBER

- If tests stress you out, they might stress out your students as well.
- Remember that *anxiety* and *stress* are very conducive to either fighting or fleeing, but not to acquiring academic content.
- Promote a desire to learn in your students by teaching them that they can be successful in school.
- Relate teaching to the interests and experiences of your students.
- Vary the types of activities you do *frequently*.
- Always tell your students how wonderful their knowledge is, not how dangerous or inadequate their knowledge deficits can be.

The reader who wants to look further into problems associated with "zero-tolerance" policies can see:

Skiba, R., Reynolds, C. R., Graham, S., Sheras, P., Conoley, J. C., & Garcia-Vazquez, E. (2006). Are zero tolerance policies effective in the schools? An evidentiary review and recommendations. Retrieved October 15, 2007, from http://www.apa.org/ed/cpse/zttfreport.pdf

10

Find the Function

A common attribute of humans is to label things. One year at a major holiday, my brother-in-law made a mealtime side dish—red cabbage cooked with apples. I tried this material and being human, succumbed to the human temptation to label it, and placed it in the category of "vile." My sister-in-law, after being directly prodded for her opinion repeatedly, smiled and said, "I'm sure that it's the kind of thing, that if I liked it, I'd *really* like it." Perfect southern lady.

We have the same tendency when it comes to behavior. If we see a behavior that we don't like or approve of or that we are unfamiliar with, we tend to label it as "bad," "odd," "immoral," and the like. However, the thing that we should keep in mind is that behavior occurs for a reason. Behavior occurs because it works for a person, at least in some setting or in some circumstance. If a behavior doesn't work for us somehow, we stop doing it. If this were not so, we couldn't adapt to our environment. So even though a behavior may look nonsensical to us, behavior serves a purpose for the child. To paraphrase the wisdom of President George W. Bush, who intoned the prophetic phrase "words mean something," we can adjust the adage slightly to formulate the slogan of anybody who works with children, which should be "behavior means something."

In other words, behavior occurs for a reason. We may not initially understand it, it may not be *even remotely logical,* but irrelevant behavior simply does not continue. And when it comes to the behavior of children, the functions that have been identified in helping explain the majority of their behavior problems can be attributed to four broad factors:

- Getting (or avoiding) attention
- Escaping from something
- Getting something
- Getting sensory stimulation of some kind

I know it sounds overly simple, but this has been the result of *thousands* of studies involving successful attempts to change disruptive, even dangerous behavior. Between graduate students that I work with and my own private work, we have done it hundreds of times. And by "it" I mean a *functional behavior assessment.* This is a process of data collection that leads to a hypothesis concerning the function that a behavior serves. If you have a good idea about why a behavior occurs, you're much more likely to be able to plan an effective behavior intervention.

Otherwise, you're left with the option of essentially pulling behavior interventions out of the sky. Admittedly, this is the way a friend of mine, who fancies himself a mechanic, goes about fixing his lawn mower. ("Okay, I put on a new carburetor and she still won't start, so I'm thinking about putting on a new solenoid. Uh, does a lawn mower have a solenoid?") By the time he figures out that what he needed all along was a $2 spark plug, he has spend $175 and invested nearly 650 hours of his time—although, from a *functional* perspective, the completed repairs took all summer so he never had to cut grass, and it would have cost him hundreds of dollars to pay somebody else to cut his grass anyway. Crazy like a fox.

But think about it—if you figure out that a student is engaging in a pattern of disruptive behaviors and that the function of the disruptive behaviors is escaping from school work, this information is critical to effective intervention planning. You would not, for example, select time out as your intervention, because you may not help at all. In fact, you could unknowingly make the behavior *worse* because the function—escaping from school work—was achieved much more efficiently, so even though your goal was to stop the behavior you inadvertently made things worse.

Consider the following example. A twelve-year-old boy was engaging in a disruptive behavior at school. By disruptive behavior, I'm not alluding to the pencil tapping, squirming in the seat stuff that we sometimes hear called "disruptive." Peanut (remember Peanut?) was really breaking bad. I'm talking about the yelling out, calling adults names, using profanity, and tearing up materials type of behavior (the kind that is normative during faculty meetings in which stern memos are being read aloud concerning the proper position to which males should return the toilet seat in the lounge restrooms, but that isn't nearly as conducive to acquiring academic content in the classroom).

During the baseline period (or the initial observation phase), the disruption was observed to occur about twenty times each day. A functional behavior assessment was done by a bright guy in my class, Chad Dollar, the results of which suggested that this student was engaging in these behaviors to get adult attention. He was getting this in the form of negative attention (reprimands) for engaging in disruptive behaviors. The intent of the teacher giving him the negative attention was to get him to stop being disruptive, not to get him to do it more. But a cycle had been created that probably followed a set of events that went something like:

- Start with the premise that attention is as surely a basic human need as food or water. If you don't believe it, close yourself up in a dark closet with ear plugs in your ears, large padded clothing, and nothing else. Now stay there for a month. Go ahead—we'll wait. If isolation from others was not aversive, why would it be a popular torture technique? I know that those of you with young children think the closet thing with no noise and interruptions and all the sleep you want sounds pretty good, but it would get old—though you might enjoy it for a couple of weeks anyway.

- A kid, in this case Peanut, is not getting the amount of attention that he developmentally needs.
- The unavailability of a basic need—attention from others—results in his engaging in some aberrant behavior(s). This phenomenon is similar to what happens, for example, when your significant other is deprived of some elemental human need (such as the remote control for the television), and aberrant behaviors emerge such as use of words that are not characteristically associated with religious gatherings, facial twitches, and hours of random ambulation through your home seeking the electronic elemental human need when this person could have manually changed the channel in seconds.
- The kid's aberrant behavior is "corrected" by the classroom teacher, giving the kid a fix that we all need.
- The kid's aberrant behavior, rather than decreasing, becomes more likely to occur, and when it does, the teacher attempts to correct it, although the result is opposite to what is intended, and so on.
- Disruptive behavior becomes the primary mechanism by which the kid gets his need for attention met, at least in the school setting, until this study, during which Peanut *never* received positive attention, only reprimands, so he was never "good," he was always disruptive.

Based on the assessment results, a simplified version of the advice given to the teacher was something like, "How's about we ignore these 'disruptions' and spend scads of time paying positive attention to him for doing the things you want him to do?"

An edited version of the response was something like, "You're full of malarkey."

So the consensus-building question was something like, "Well, what do you think we should do?"

And the predictable response was something like, "I'm going to get in his face every time he messes up."

So our ostensibly defeated reply was, "Well, if you're absolutely going to reprimand him for being disruptive regardless of what the data suggest, can you do one thing? Can you make *absolutely sure* to reprimand him *every single time* that he does something you don't want him to do? We'll just watch."

Which leads to phase 1, where the teacher fussed at him *every time he was disruptive,* where she was truly committed to excellence in implementing the plan, where the disruptive behavior more than doubled, and where we tittered like debutantes at our coming out ball, but did so in an unobtrusive and professional way. After this phase, which could technically be called a functional analysis, there was more flexibility about considering the intervention originally proposed. Thus was implemented phase 2, *involving only giving attention for desirable behaviors and ignoring disruptive behaviors,* which resulted in about a 50% reduction in disruption from the baseline period. The results were good, but not optimal, so a very simple token system was added in phase 3. The token system provided the student with opportunities to earn some preferred activities after his work was finished and if his behavior was "good," which led to the observation that the disruptive behavior no longer could be observed at all. This observance of no observance was maintained for the school year. The results are presented in the following graph, and no, they are not made up.

As I sit here rubbing congratulatory calluses on my own back, I am drawn up short by a sudden realization. A four-legged mammal whose intellectual capacity I have in

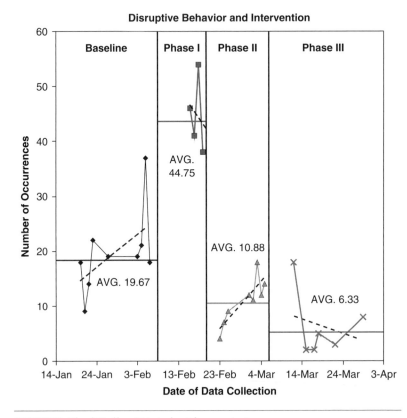

Disruptive Behavior and Intervention

SOURCE: Chad Dollar. Printed with permission.

the past suggested was on par with a highly processed food product, whom I rescued from certain demise from the dog pound, who should have been grateful for the privilege of residing in my backyard, has managed to not only take up residence *inside my home* but also make me feel supremely intelligent and magnanimous if she limits herself to voiding her bladder on my carpet only a couple of times (or approximately 3½ gallons) a day. I guess that any of us can miss the forest for the trees. If only she would see the potential in those trees that her canine cousins see. And with this brief introduction, know that you will hear of my dog Bumpus again in Chapter 22.

POINTS TO REMEMBER

- Behavior occurs for a reason. If behavior does not serve a purpose or function, it goes away.
- Even though classroom behaviors can be disruptive, disturbing, even scary, research has shown that most childhood behavioral difficulties serve one of (or a combination of) four functions: (1) to get (or avoid) attention, (2) to escape from something (like undesirable school assignments), (3) to get something tangible, or (4) self-stimulation (humming, tapping).
- Data collection procedures have been developed to identify the function of a behavior. These are subsumed under the heading *functional behavior assessment.*
- The great thing about functional behavior assessment is that it leads to intervention planning. The great thing about interventions based on such assessments is you will know pretty quickly if you really identified the function of the student's behavior—the plan will work!
- The outcome of this process is that intervention planning is typically much more efficient than when using the strategy of simply "pulling interventions out of the air."

An exceptional review of functional behavior assessment was done by:

Hanley, G. P., Iwata, B. A., & McCord, B. E. (2003). Functional analysis of problem behavior: A review. *Journal of Applied Behavior Analysis, 36,* 147–185.

A very good step-by-step guide to actually conducting a functional behavior assessment is:

Oneil, R. E., Horner, R. H., Albin, R. W., Sprague, J. R., Storey, K., & Newton, J. S. (1997). *Functional assessment and program development for problem behavior: A practical handbook* (2nd ed.). Boston: Brooks Cole.

And if you happen to think that children's behavior doesn't occur because it serves a function, but they act the way they do because they are scheming to take over the world Children-of-the-Corn style, you definitely need to read and memorize:

Department of the Army. (2006). *Counterinsurgency.* Washington, DC: Author. Retrieved October 15, 2007, from http://usacac.army.mil/CAC/Repository/Materials/ USA-USMCCOINNewsRelease.pdf

And for heaven's sake, eat it after you read it!

Don't Be an Old Yeller

There is really nothing that causes us, and I am referring here to the true American pioneer spirit, to salute our heritage with misty eyes and thankful heart, like a sad movie. What movie tugs at the heart strings more than *Old Yeller?* The faithful friend and companion who works with us, lives with us, and ultimately sacrifices his life for our own. What a great American classic.

Unfortunately, sometimes in the school setting, you can find another kind of *old yeller,* one not nearly as endearing— the teacher who resorts to yelling at students as a behavior management tool. In fact, my first job working with children was in a preschool setting. One of the teachers was known to have the best-behaved class, and I went to observe. She managed behavior primarily by yelling. She didn't *bellow,* I didn't consider her behavior child abuse, but she did yell. A lot. And these four-year-olds did comply with her outbursts. But let's consider some of the downsides of being an old yeller.

Most of us, whether teachers, mental health people, or camp counselors, would agree that one of the (if not *the*) major jobs that children have is to *learn.* We want kids to learn— survival skills, safety skills, social skills, academic skills.

However, if you have been alive for more than a month or two, you know that there are disparities that exist between different groups of students on a variety of measures that we use to assess learning, such as the intelligence quotient (IQ).

A couple of researchers investigated the question of disparities in IQ and found some really interesting things. They compared the homes of children growing up with parents who were professional and financially secure to the homes of children whose parents were receiving public assistance. By the age of three, children with professional parents had an average IQ of 117, and children with parents living in poverty had an IQ of 79. Rather than assuming this difference was inborn, they found that:

- Financially secure parents directed an average of 487 utterances to their children, compared to 178 directed to the children in poverty.
- By the time their children reached age three, the parents on public assistance directed 200,000 statements of prohibition/disapproval and 80,000 positive/approval statements toward their children, while the financially secure/educated parents had directed 80,000 negative statements and 500,000 positive statements to their children.

The point of mentioning this is not to inspire prejudicial feelings toward anyone. I do hope that you draw a couple of inferences from this research. First, early exposure to stimuli such as language—particularly positive feedback—may greatly enhance academic achievement. The second inference that I think you can make is that some of the children you see that are not being successful may have already had more than their share of negative feedback. Many students may already be "primed" to expect failure in a lot of the things they do, and old yellers can quickly demonstrate to children that they are not going to be successful in the school environment.

In my "professional" life, or my life of working with children, I have received three pieces of feedback that really meant a lot to me. The first one was by the grandfather/caregiver of a student I worked with who told me that he was glad I was working with his kid because he could tell that I had worked before. As a former miner and construction worker, I really appreciated the sentiment. The second piece was given to me by the father of a student that I had worked with who told me that every time he saw me, he thought of the following line from an Austin Powers movie, "I didn't spend six years in Evil Medical School to be called MISTER, thank you very much." That one speaks for itself.

The final piece of feedback that I have valued is the letter that was read on television. It was written by an elementary school student (his mother swore it was his idea and work) to nominate me for a local television award called "My Teacher Is Tops." I received the award based on his nomination. People from the television station showed up in the classroom unannounced with a video camera—I thought it was a *60 Minutes* exposé (I always thought I was a bit unconventional). They read the letter of nomination and gave me the award. I noted how important it was that I had set a goal for myself not to succumb to the temptation of being an old yeller since it was among the first things he wrote in the nomination letter.

> I think that "my teacher is tops" because, he never raises his voice or push us or rush us to hurry and do our work, he's very patient and calm, he's always listening to us also. He will let us catch up when we are behind.

> Mr. Waller trys his very best to take us outside everyday to let us let out our anger, or friendship. I love when he reads to us. I'm very greatfull that he is my teacher for many reasons. I can't expess them all on paper. And thats a few reasons I think "my teacher is Tops."

POINTS TO REMEMBER

- Talk to them.
- Read to them.
- Teach them.
- Tell them your expectations.
- DON'T YELL DURING ANY OF THESE ACTIVITIES!

The reader who is interested in environmental differences and the effect these differences might have on IQ should see:

Hart, B., & Risley, T. (1995). *Meaningful differences in the everyday experience of young American children.* Baltimore, MD: Paul H. Brookes.

12

Let Them Eat Cake—If It Reinforces Their Behavior

Probably the most common misunderstanding among teachers and other adults who work with children is the idea of *reinforcement*. All of us use the term and think it is integral to the teaching process, but many of us are confused about what it truly means to *reinforce*. You don't reinforce a *person*; you reinforce a *behavior* with some *reinforcer*. The word *reinforcer* is even heard in our popular culture, but to give you an example of how integrated the concept is, the word processing program that I am currently using does not recognize the word *reinforcer*, yet it *did* recognize the word *malarkey* from Chapter 10. Go figure.

Years ago I was in the military and stationed in Germany. While there, I went out to eat at a restaurant with a woman who was also in the military. One thing I learned on this date is that people in Germany will apparently pay a huge number of play-looking currency notes for an appetizer that has a fancy name, but that even the casual observer whose date orders this menu item because he is paying can see that, when the item actually arrives at the table, the ingredients include melted butter, toasted white bread, and *bugs*. Do not read ANY further until you internalize the significance of this; there were, on a plate across from me, creatures that *I had paid for*, the presence of which would have resulted in a lowered health rating in a restaurant in my home country. As badly as I wanted to curry the favor of my date by demonstrating my cosmopolitan palate, I simply couldn't get past the problem that the appetizer that I had purchased, and which my date consumed with gusto, looked exactly like the appetizer's cousins which I frequently cleaned out of my dog's water dish. I vividly remember seeing two distinct antennae protruding from their torsos as she crunched open the shells. She tried several times to entice me to sample the appetizer, telling me how delicious the garlic toast garnish was, prompting me to ponder:

- If the garlic toast is so tasty, I'll eat garlic toast sans the gastropods.
- Garlic toast is *much* cheaper than broiled, slime-trailing bugs.
- I need to completely reconsider ideas that I might have about smooching on the first date (or any date involving bug consumption).

Clearly, the availability of seasoned bugs on toast *reinforced* my date's appetizer-eating behavior. Equally as clearly, it did not reinforce any of my behavior, which leads to a vital point about reinforcement. What confuses many people is that *reinforcement* is a behavioral term, not an intuitive term. In other words, reinforcement is determined by the effect that something has on behavior. If you present something following a targeted behavior and your target behavior *increases*, you have reinforced that behavior. I sometimes hear people say about a child they are working with, "I tried that reinforcement stuff but it just didn't work." On further investigation (and without quibbling over the inaccuracy of that statement), what that person did was offer candy, tokens, or something similar to entice a student to do something (like complete a math worksheet). The kid didn't complete the boring work, hence the statement "reinforcement just didn't work."

Remember, though, reinforcement is not necessarily intuitive; it's not required to be practical; it's behavioral. Sure, lots of students will do a boring math sheet for a piece of candy. Lots of kids will do it just because you ask them to. You can rest assured, though, that Peanut (who has the perfect kid name but also, as we saw in Chapter 10, has a few "issues") will snort derisively at the offer and throw the offending worksheet in the trash can. You *did not* reinforce Peanut's worksheet-completing behavior. It can become more convoluted when you want to use something like verbal praise as a reinforcer, because when you spout off a hearty "good job" to Peanut from across the classroom after noticing him apparently focusing on an assigned task in an attempt to reinforce his behavior—your comment may have the effect of completely breaking his train of thought and reminding him that he would rather be spitting chunks of paper at another kid (because your "reinforcement" might be referred to by Peanut as a "distraction" or an "interruption").

So how do you figure out what will reinforce the behavior of a specific kid? It can be tricky. There are some good bets. Kids of all ages are likely to be reinforced by the opportunity to move. You can be pretty confident that your attention will be a reinforcer for younger children. I'll tell you a secret if you promise not to tell. The older kids want your attention too, even if they do look at you like you spent too many of your own teenage years inhaling the fumes of burning milk jugs when you praise them. It's true that the older students are really starting to play for the attention of their friends, too, so they are basically torn between wanting your positive attention and the attention of their peers.

Another trick that you can try to identify reinforcers for children is: ask them. They often (though not always) can give good insight into what will reinforce their behavior early in the process of developing your behavior plan. It is *always* a good idea to ask any group of students what they would be interested in earning. Sometimes you will get information that isn't very useful. For example, sometimes a child will tell you something that they would like to have the opportunity to earn because they like the *idea* of it, but when access is finally possible, it just doesn't seem to inspire them. This phenomenon, not specific to children, helps explain why you can buy exercise equipment cheap at any yard sale.

Sometimes you will be told things that are grossly beyond reason and reach, similar to the idea that any of us born after about 1950 will actually draw Social Security retirement benefits. But even when the information is unreasonable, it might give you something that you can work with. For example, one teenager that I was working with suggested he might be willing to do his school work if I bought him a car (he obviously hadn't seen what I drove), but finding out that he had an interest in cars led me to bring in some auto repair manuals from home. We incorporated reading repair manuals into the assignments, which he would do, and I let him earn the opportunity to go with me out to my car after his doing a specified amount of assigned work, where I would show him different parts of a car and tell him how they work.

Another way that you can try to figure out what will reinforce the behavior of a specific child is to watch her. Most people, given some freedom to choose what they are going to do (and this is way out there, so hold on) will choose something they *like.* And it can be a little wacky. I have seen kids who would start to do math for the first time in the school year to earn the opportunity to *push the wall.* I have seen kids that were reinforced by the opportunity *to follow rules* (as an anecdotal note, this is something that I have seen a couple of times in kids with Asperger syndrome or with high functioning autism—not a research-based statement, just a casual observation). In these cases, if students will work for rules, *give 'em some rules!* But be fair; don't give them rules that make it overly hard on them just because their behavior is reinforced by rule-following. I have seen kids with severe disabilities who were reinforced by watching a few seconds of Barney, such that, long after I wanted to beat myself into sweet oblivion with a blunt object, they would still work to see that unending purple dream (or nightmare). Behavioral, not intuitive.

Do not think that you should limit yourself by offering to make available only a few reinforcers. Variety is the spice of life. Think about it—why do you go to work day after day? Yeah, yeah, the higher calling of educating the masses, blah, blah. But most of us have to admit, at least on some level, that money reinforces our coming to work behavior. Why does money work so well? Because you can buy all kinds of stuff with it. If all that you could buy with money was a trip to the treasure bucket, I dare prophesy that your work attendance would suffer. Even if you really love chocolate more than life itself, if money could only be used to buy M&Ms, after some point of gluttonous "melts in your mouth but not in your hands" consumption, you might surprise yourself by thinking something like, "Well, gosh, I find myself, for some reason, with a craving for a juicy cut of some meat—medium well—or maybe I'll indulge in a plateful of bugs."

After you identify reinforcers, implement a simple system that will give your students control over access to the rein-forcers at a rate of frequency that works for them. It's time to face the facts; most school-aged children—and I'm including high schoolers here—simply have not developed the ability to delay gratification, such as waiting until the end of the semes-ter for a party, or until the end of the week for a little free time. A lot of them won't be able to wait until the *end of the day*. Lest you get too judgmental, I would remind you of this: years ago in many school systems, teachers received ten paychecks per year, not the twelve that is standard now. Teachers were expected to budget their ten checks such that they would last through the summer, whereas today most teachers receive twelve paychecks but still only work for ten months. Apparently, however, numerous observant school system superintendents noticed that, by the end of the summer, their teaching staff could frequently be found at interstate off-ramps offering to teach for food. Preferably pastry products.

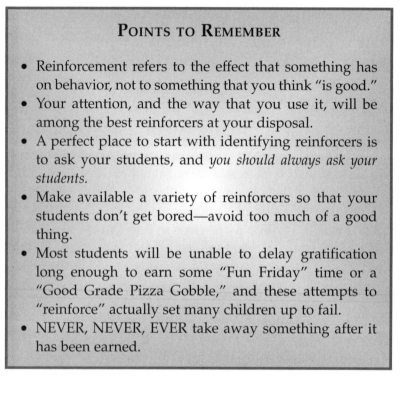

POINTS TO REMEMBER

- Reinforcement refers to the effect that something has on behavior, not to something that you think "is good."
- Your attention, and the way that you use it, will be among the best reinforcers at your disposal.
- A perfect place to start with identifying reinforcers is to ask your students, and *you should always ask your students*.
- Make available a variety of reinforcers so that your students don't get bored—avoid too much of a good thing.
- Most students will be unable to delay gratification long enough to earn some "Fun Friday" time or a "Good Grade Pizza Gobble," and these attempts to "reinforce" actually set many children up to fail.
- NEVER, NEVER, EVER take away something after it has been earned.

The reader who is interested in ideas for classroom reinforcers—and tons of other good ideas—should definitely check out a Web site put together by a school psychologist named Jim Wright at:

http://www.interventioncentral.org

13

Nurturing

Something that parents, teachers, and others often say to me (or within earshot of me) is that they are concerned that they will reward (or reinforce) kids too much. It's true that, if your home is anything like mine, then Toys 'R' Occupying More Living Space Than 'U' 'R.' Or, as a dad responded to me when I recently asked about the holidays, "my kids have a hard time distinguishing between Christmas and any other day of the year." When I was a kid, everything that I owned fit neatly into a box that, even when it contained every earthly possession that I could claim, still held an air pocket big enough to keep David Blaine alive for a week underwater. It's no surprise that many people would have concerns about rewarding children too much when you consider the relative "plenty" that we enjoy.

It's also not surprising that people have concerns about "over-rewarding" because a lot of people don't understand precisely what is meant by *reinforcing* a child. *Reinforcement* is a term thrown around a lot, but not always correctly (as discussed in the previous chapter), and nobody wants to *spoil* his child. A related concept that is hurled around frequently is *nurturing*. Sometimes people, when discussing children, include terms like *natural consequences, tough love*, and things of that ilk. If you look up the word *nurture* in a dictionary, one of the definitions provided will be something like "sustenance, the things needed to help grow." That is the nurture that we need to be talking about in relation to children. And the good news (especially for you beginning teachers, who have to call home collect to ask for quarters to do your laundry—if you can afford any clothes) is that nurturing doesn't cost a thing. No Tickle Me Goober doll needed.

Children need food to grow. We all know that, even if we don't see enough nutritional value in the standard toaster creamy sugar roll breakfast product to maintain basic life functions in a firefly. Usually (but too far from *always*), kids in the United States have food. Thankfully, hunger has been eliminated here. I know this because the U.S. Department of Agriculture (USDA) says so. Unfortunately, some people (and *way* too many kids) are what the USDA calls *food insecure.* I hope you can see the difference.

It's harder to measure whether children are "nurture starved." However, even if children are nurture *gorged* at home, it's no more reasonable to ask them to, say, go to school all day long without receiving any nurturing than it would be to expect them to go to school all day without receiving any food (and yes, the offerings in the cafeteria technically count as food). Beyond the school doors, though, more and more kids are in afterschool programs and various activities—many of which may not provide much nurturing. More children are growing up in homes in which all caregivers are wage earners, and sometimes work stresses (including the nurture-starvation of adults) interfere with the nurturing of children. In any case, I think it's safe to assume that the number of children at risk for ego obesity from overindulgent nurturance consumption is small.

While it is clearly immoral and unethical to intentionally withhold nurturing from children to measure the direct effects, nurturance deprivation has been studied in animals. Some of you, in fact, may remember the experiments of Harry Harlow. Harlow began investigating what he called "contact comfort," and found that baby monkeys (that had been removed from their mothers) preferred (needed) the nurturance of the comforting touch of a soft, terry cloth surrogate mother. In fact, they consistently preferred the soft surrogate terry cloth "mom" to a wire surrogate that provided the baby monkeys with food. Harlow further investigated the monkeys' need for nurturing by having the soft surrogate mom squirt cold water on or poke the baby monkeys with spikes, and the monkeys still preferred the soft, abusive surrogate mother to the wire mother that provided food. I hope that those of you who may have snorted derisively at my comparing the need for nurturance with the need for food have noticed that the need for nurturance in these baby monkeys *outweighed their need for wire-surrogate-administered food.*

What does this mean to you? Postpone any lemon sucking that you do until all contact with children is finished for the day. As soon as you see a child, *smile.* They need you to smile at them, even if they tell you not to (teenagers). *Speak to them*—a lot. Pat them on the back or ruffle their hair (but *not* teenagers)—a lot. Keep track of how often you do this *for every single kid* that you are around. It is really easy to unintentionally do these things more for one kid than another—and the kids will know! When working with parents, I often say that we should set a goal that they will touch—in a positive way—their child. The parent will often smirk and ask how often, and I'll say something like ten times each hour.

Caregivers will typically laugh the laugh of the truly patronizing, assure me that they already do way more than that, but to make me feel good about myself, they will usually agree to keep data on their "nurturing behavior" for a week. When I see them again, they are usually no longer giggling. They are tired. They say that they never realized how *hard* it is to give ten positive touches per hour. Again, this is not surprising. We really intend to do these things, we often think that we have followed through on our good intentions—but we often haven't.

POINTS TO REMEMBER

- Give compliments to ALL of your students.
- Smile at and talk to ALL of your students.
- Don't ever stop doing the two points listed above.

The reader who is interested in jumping head first into some of the studies about the monkey babies may want to start in the beginning with:

Harlow, H. F. (1958). The nature of love. *American Psychologist, 13,* 673–685.

For further discussion on Harlow's work (and the effect it may have had on him), an excellent book is:

Slater, L. (2004). *Opening Skinner's box: Great psychological experiments of the twentieth century.* New York: Norton.

And last but not least, anyone wanting to learn more about food insecurity can read:

Williamson, E. (2006, November 16). Some Americans lack food, but USDA won't call them hungry. *Washington Post,* p. A01.

Bag It, but Don't Tag It

In my own work with children, I often hear them described in a variety of ways. "I never had this type of trouble with your brother," or "None of my friend's children embarrass their parents in public," or "This kid needs Sunday school more than any kid here and he won't listen," or "These are my lower readers," or "That kid is b-a-d," or "He knows exactly what he's doing and he's doing it on purpose." To their credit, the same people making statements like these typically would not tolerate another person making a similar comment. What a terrible weight it must be for a child to bear the burden of "the worst" or "the least," of being "in the low group," or just "not quite good enough."

I think that most of us can agree, though, that all children—in fact, all people—want to be good at something. So what happens to a student who hears or senses that she is inferior or unable? Maybe being the best at being the worst is a logical choice for a child who perceives that she is never going to reach your expectations. Rather than fading into tepid obscurity, why not be the class clown, or the rebel, or the troublemaker?

I have also heard a variety of explanations offered to elucidate why a student may be doing a specific undesirable behavior. One of my favorite explanations is "he's just being manipulative," as if being manipulative is a bad thing. Are we not being manipulative when we adjust the thermostat in our home? Put another way, are we not attempting to manipulate the climate of our home so that the environment is more tolerable to us? Yes, students are sometimes "manipulative" in that they are trying to make the school environment more tolerable or comfortable by engaging in some behavior that we might find undesirable.

Another classic descriptor of undesirable behavior I often hear is "he knows exactly what he's doing." I concede that a strong argument can be made that, if a student engages in a particular behavior then he, in fact, knows he engaged in that behavior. My response, as a highly trained mental health professional, is usually "so what?" Just because you know the speed limit doesn't translate to your driving at the speed limit. Smokers know that they smoke—even if they badly want *not* to smoke. It seems to me that the primary outcome of explaining the behavior of children in ways like "they are being manipulative" or "they know what they are doing" is that children become described or perceived by adults in a negative way. And if we perceive students in a negative way, they will know it. And instead of helping the child, the label often seems to serve as an end in itself, providing an excuse *not* to intervene rather than giving a road map to intervention.

One of the most famous stories in the mental health world is the story of Clever Hans. Clever Hans was a horse that achieved fame in the late 1800s for his ability to compute simple math problems. Clever Hans was tested by scientist after scientist (probably physicists), with each one concluding that Clever Hans could do what was claimed. Eventually however, after careful observations, a researcher named Oskar Pfungst made a couple of important discoveries: when no one questioning Hans knew the right answer to a math problem (probably physicists), Hans missed the answer, too, and when

Hans couldn't see the questioner, he answered incorrectly. Pfungst definitively showed that Hans was actually *picking up on unconscious bodily cues* being given off by the questioner, and that he could not, in fact, do math computations. So Hans, we would probably agree, was on the Mr. Ed end of horse intelligence, but a mathematician he was not.

A similar phenomenon has been implicated in such things as the Ouija board and divining rods. Using the example of divining rods: there are people who are absolutely convinced that they can take a Y-shaped stick and use it to find underground water supplies. The people with the sticks are sometimes called *dowsers*. Those who believe that the people with the sticks can actually find water are sometimes called *gullible*. And I feel confident that at least some of the dowsers are quite convinced that they are engaging in some mythical practice that leads them to water. Be that as it may, systematic research has shown that you or I can actually locate water (at random) *more accurately* than the dowsers, who are not responding to mythical power pointing to underground water, but are actually responding to what is called the *ideomotor effect*.

The mind is a powerful thing. It can convince us of things that aren't really true (sorry, but the prediction that the Ouija board made about the name of your future spouse is no better than my prediction that your future spouse will be named Peanut). The mind can even provide us with information that the conveyor doesn't mean to convey or, through misinterpretation by another person, can be thought to convey something that wasn't really there. If you communicate that a kid is "bad" in the teacher's lounge, there is a good chance that you are communicating it to the kid in the classroom, too, just not verbally. Not convinced? I also know that people have a tendency to know what we *really think* about them, regardless of *what we say*. And I also know that beauty is in the eye of the beholder, and *it's a good thing that it is,* and if you look deeply enough, you can see the humanity in the eyes of any child. Or adult. And don't be deceived about your students' ability to read the body language that you convey about how you feel about them. After all, it seems insulting to acknowledge that a horse can accurately interpret a person's body language and to think that a child cannot.

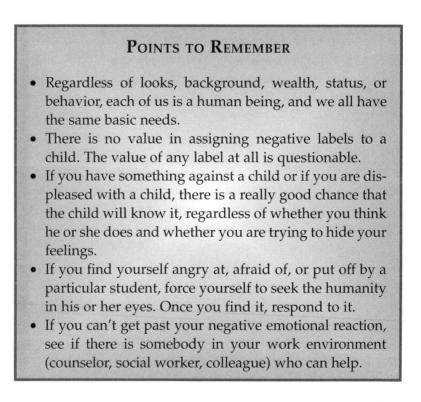

POINTS TO REMEMBER

- Regardless of looks, background, wealth, status, or behavior, each of us is a human being, and we all have the same basic needs.
- There is no value in assigning negative labels to a child. The value of any label at all is questionable.
- If you have something against a child or if you are displeased with a child, there is a really good chance that the child will know it, regardless of whether you think he or she does and whether you are trying to hide your feelings.
- If you find yourself angry at, afraid of, or put off by a particular student, force yourself to seek the humanity in his or her eyes. Once you find it, respond to it.
- If you can't get past your negative emotional reaction, see if there is somebody in your work environment (counselor, social worker, colleague) who can help.

The reader who is interested in Clever Hans and Ouija boards may want to review:

Randi, J. (1995). *An Encyclopedia of Claims, Frauds, and Hoaxes of the Occult and Supernatural.* James Randi Educational Foundation. Retrieved October 2, 2007, from http://www.randi.org/encyclopedia/Clever%20Hans%20 phenomenon.html

15

You Say
"Tomato," I Say
"Abnormal"

A dult humans seem to forget the things that they did, felt, and thought when they themselves were children. One result is that, when adults observe children doing the same type of thing that they probably did as children, the adults are likely to assume that the best explanation for the children's behavioral manifestation is demonic possession. Children engaging in conversations about sex or using profanity are two things that are strong evidence, the average adult seems to assume, that an offending child is having direct conversations with Beelzebub. Usually, though, when we think *way* back, we may spark a distant memory, long buried, of a time that as a child, we too laughed at a lunchtime belch until milk was ejected from our nose.

The process by which we adults lose our childhood memories involves a physiological degeneration of the brain that is slowly progressive. This deterioration has impacted the average adult so significantly that, by the time her own child becomes a teenager, the mass of the adult brain is reduced so dramatically that, if the stricken adult shakes her head vigorously, all teenagers within two blocks can actually hear the adult brain rattling about in the adult skull. Teens tell me that the sound is similar to what you would expect to hear made by the vigorous shaking of an Ensure can containing a pebble, and they call the physiological brain shriveling "getting old." A particularly extreme case of getting old is referred to as "parenthood."

I am going to relate an occurrence from my own childhood that I hope will obviate some of your adult amnesic-inspired concerns. I remember vividly a classroom group project episode that occurred when I was in the fourth grade. My group was comprised entirely of males, each of whom was a personal friend. The assignment involved our looking through magazines that the teacher had brought in from home and cutting out pictures that we used to make a poster that explained the theme of the academic subject that we were studying—whatever that was.

My group completed this challenging academic task in approximately four seconds. We spent the rest of the allotted time, about three hours, I think, looking through magazines to find pictures of cleavage. When we found such pictures, which sported approximately three millimeters of cleavage in those days, we tittered excitedly while breaking out in prepubescent sweat, and spoke to one another in hushed tones (and I realize here that I am completely conceding any hope of ever again being a viable competitor for inspiring the mating instinct in another human) of "teeter-totters." The train of deduction that led to our labeling a part of the human body as a term reserved for a piece of playground equipment, or that sounds similar to a processed potato side dish, I can't say. Nor do I have any recollection whatsoever of the academic content that was covered on that day.

While this admission might seem somewhat quaint (or somewhat disturbing) to you, I assure you that this episode, had our conversation been overheard or our activities observed, would have been explained by adults as possession by demons of the most nefarious variety and would have subsequently resulted in the immediate lifting of our bodies by the fleshy parts of our ears and our receiving lobe-assisted transportation to the principal's office. After several punitive interventions were applied and psychological assessments conducted, a school assembly of all students would have been convened in the auditorium to discuss how each one of us offenders would undoubtedly, as a result of our perversion, be consigned to a career field that embarrassed our parents and probably required completion of a jurist doctorate.

There is something of an unspoken hierarchy of behavioral problems that adults expect to see in children. At a certain point on this hierarchy, many adults think that the behavioral problem morphs into a character or morality issue. One set of behaviors that commonly represents the morphing point for many adults is when children, particularly young children, engage in the use of profanity and/or violate established parameters for sexual expression or behavior. I confess there is something slightly unsettling about hearing a six-year-old child use language that is akin to the language that my drill instructor used to describe my heritage. There is something bothersome about hearing a child in kindergarten speak in sexually explicit terms, or observing one child touch another student inappropriately.

The point that we need to remember, though, is that these manifestations are *behavioral* issues, just like the manifestation of other undesirable behaviors that we may see. Exposure, through various means, to increasingly graphic images, sounds, ideas, and the like means that their repetition by children in the classroom is more likely. It also means that language and sexuality may be expressed by children in ways that, while becoming more acceptable in popular culture, continue to be considered contrary to the school setting. The result is that, as teachers, we might find ourselves educating the role of context in behavior. Put another way, we may have to communicate to children the idea that behavior that is acceptable (or allowable) in one setting may not be acceptable in another.

Yes, the role of context in behavior is a useful thing to teach, and involves a skill set that we practice all the time. Some behaviors that are fine for poker night wouldn't be quite as functional in a religious ceremony. There are things that we might say in the teacher's lounge that we might not say in class (although we shouldn't get carried away in the teacher's lounge). And there may be things that children (unfortunately) hear or see on television, or from parents, or from friends or siblings that are acceptable (in that they are permitted), but these may *not* be okay at school.

This disparity between various acceptable standards in different settings can be completely novel—and confusing— to your students. Move gently. Be careful of overreaction, because overreaction could place a child in the position of having his caregiver on one side and you on another, with the child in the middle. Assume that children don't know that they have violated your expectations, and teach acceptable standards in your setting. If you react in a strongly negative manner, you may be assigning your negative emotional response to something that a caregiver has allowed—not a good situation for you or for a child. And it often penalizes a child for you to assume that he "knows better," when in fact he may *not* know better. And a strong reaction might actually encourage the child to do the same thing again.

Years ago, I worked in a residential facility that was an alternative placement for teenagers who, because of illegal behavior, would have otherwise been placed in Youth Development Centers. We required that these boys (all of whom were sixteen or seventeen years old) shave daily because part of the program involved their working with the public. When I first started working there, I noticed that the boys frequently got in trouble for not shaving. I walked in their bathroom one morning, thinking that I might catch them horse playing instead of getting ready for work. One boy was holding shaving cream in one hand and a razor in another, looking back and forth between the two. I asked him if there was a problem, and he said that it hurt when he shaved.

I asked him to tell me how he shaved, and it immediately became clear that he really had no idea how to denude the six hairs he sported proudly on his face without also removing the majority of his face. When I started to teach him, every other boy in the program magically appeared and wanted to hear the lesson. In this forum, they admitted that *not one of them had ever been taught to shave*. For some reason, maybe embarrassment, the boys continued to get in trouble rather than say that they simply didn't know how to shave. That idea had simply not occurred to me.

Just in case things don't seem complicated enough, certain displays of sexuality could indicate that a child has been mal-treated in some manner. A young child who touches herself in class may be engaging in normal exploration, or the child may have been the target of sexual maltreatment. It's a good idea to discuss any concerns you have with a school counselor, social worker, or psychologist. If maltreatment is suspected, follow your school's protocol for reporting this suspicion to the appropriate authority.

Don't forget, though, that children today may demonstrate unacceptable behaviors resulting from exposure to a variety of information that is beyond their maturity and that surpasses their developmental skills in handling. This provides us with many opportunities to teach that are beyond what we may have thought we would confront in the classroom. However, viewing inappropriate language use and accelerated sexual expression (depending on the circumstances) as moral prob-lems does not help effectively address the behaviors, may put us at odds with standards that have been accepted by care-givers, and can lead to our making unfair—not to mention unhelpful—assumptions about children. As society continues to find acceptable words, images, and behaviors that are unac-ceptable in the school setting, children are often left to suffer the confusion and consequences. Hopefully, we will soon begin to address the problem that some things, especially sex-ualization, once released from the box, are difficult (if not impossible) to put back.

Points to Remember

- Children today are often exposed to words, images, and other stimuli that are beyond their maturational ability to handle and that are unacceptable in the school setting.
- When children manifest behaviors resulting from exposure to inappropriate material, give them the benefit of the doubt. Assume that they don't know appropriate standards of what is acceptable to you. Then teach acceptable standards.
- If their behavior occurs in a manner that may put other children at risk, *get help immediately.* Safety always comes first and is your responsibility.
- Some expressions of sexual behavior could be suggestive of child maltreatment. Discuss any concerns you have with appropriate school personnel, and follow school policy if a report to additional authority is appropriate.
- Teach children your expectations, and you may need to teach that some words or behaviors are allowed in some settings but are not allowed in others.

The reader who is interested in ways in which a child's environment is becoming increasingly complex and challenging should read the classic:

Bronfenbrenner, U., McClelland, P., Wethington, E., Moen, P., & Ceci, S. J. (1996). *The state of Americans.* New York: Free Press.

Anyone who works with children may, at some point, have a concern that a child under his or her supervision has been maltreated. In such a case, that person will find a phenomenal resource in:

Crosson-Tower, C. (2005). *Understanding child abuse and neglect* (6th ed.). Boston: Pearson.

Any reader who thinks that my fourth-grade buddies and I were not normal, but were in fact juvenile delinquents, may agree with the following, composed by my nine-year-old poet laureate daughter, Emily (and I find that I agree more and more, as my daughters approach dating age):

Boys   Emily

Boys are cockroaches. They both are gross.

Boys are comedians. They both are silly.

Boys are flies. They both are annoying.

Boys are lions. They both are loud.

16

Positive Power of the Group

I think that one of the things that frustrates me, and a lot of people that talk to me, about education is that a lot of the macro-level policies might be nicely described as goofy. These policies often, if not always, start with a good idea, but they sometimes have unintended consequences that are undesirable. A policy illustrative of that idea was Aid to Families with Dependent Children, a program commonly referred to as "welfare." This started off with a really good idea—something like "it sure does stink to think about moms and kids starving to death." After being implemented, however, it was found that the program had some unintended consequences, such as potentially encouraging dependence rather than autonomy. It wasn't that these consequences were unforeseeable; they simply were unforeseen.

On a smaller, more personal level, I can offer the following example of how ideas can have unintended consequences. One day while driving my car and attempting to actually see the road in front of me, it occurred to me that the removal of dirt and road debris from my windshield might help me to see both the road and other objects ahead. I pushed the button that activates the pump that squirts liquid on my windshield and simultaneously activates the rubber blades that wipe the liquid, and presumably the dirt, away. However, a paltry dribble of liquid came forth that was woefully inadequate to the task of cleaning the windshield, a stream strongly resembling the desiccated trickle of ideas flowing from the average committee meeting.

When I got home, I opened the hood of my car, thinking that the washer reservoir had run empty. I discovered that such was not the case—there was plenty of washer fluid. Apparently the little jets from which the liquid was supposed to squirt had become clogged. I pondered this puzzler briefly and had a flash of genius. I have heard that you can run white vinegar through a coffee machine to clean it out. So I removed the fluid from the reservoir and filled it with white vinegar. I was about to test my genius, when I was called to the phone. Thus distracted, I completely forgot about what I had done.

I did not recall my innovation until the next time that I entered my vehicle and felt that it would be once again helpful to see the road in front of my vehicle. Coincidentally, on this trip I was accompanied by coworkers. I must say that my invention seems to have worked extremely well. When I pushed the button to squirt the wiper fluid, I was initially rewarded only by the same pitiful trickle that had sputtered forth the last time I had pushed the button. The white vinegar, however, quickly cleaned out the mechanism because the turgid trickle rapidly became a roaring river bursting forth on my windshield. My idea had worked! That is the positive side of my idea. The unintended consequence of my idea was that my coworkers began to ask when I had spilled a jar of pickles in my car. (Incidentally, pickle smell does not evaporate, it must be washed off.) I found that this washing was facilitated by ongoing smart aleck remarks from coworkers, who had *better hope* that they never wake up to find that I have become their supervisor.

Peer pressure is a powerful thing. As children age, they naturally seek more social interaction with peers rather than less, further strengthening the impact of the social group.

Adults, not being the complete dolts that children assume adults to be, have figured out the power of peer interactions. In some cases, the power of peers has been used in a negative way, and has involved things like punishing a group based on the behavior of one child, embarrassing a child in front of the group, and other permutations.

Undoubtedly, the assumption leading adults to consider strategies using group pressure to reduce undesirable behavior in one student or a small group of students is that our "favored" group will whip the "deviant" kid into shape, essentially taking care of our classroom behavioral concerns for us. Surely, there are people who have used this type of approach and may even report that it works. However, it does not give due consideration to the unintentional consequences that can occur. The unintended consequences of using the group as a disciplinary tool, unlike the unintended consequences of many governmental policies and many of my ideas, are actually known to look something like this.

Children get a lot of cues about how *they* should behave by observing how *we* behave. Admittedly, some are better at picking up cues from us than others, but observing us and observing each other is a primary mechanism by which children acquire a lot of social behavior. Incidentally, some are better models of appropriate behavior than others. If we identify a student or a small subgroup of students as not meeting our expectations, it's not hard to get the larger group to ostracize the smaller group. That doesn't mean, however, that it's a natural step for the "undesirable" student to automatically acquire the desirable behavior. In fact, it's unlikely that this type of negative peer attention will, by itself, foster the acquisition of desired behaviors or skills.

If the unlikely *does* occur and an ostracized child does pick up the desired behavior, that doesn't *in any way* imply that the isolated student will, after rising to our expectations, then be welcomed back into the "desirable" fold with open arms from forgiving hearts. Once a child is identified negatively, once a child is ostracized by peers (or adults), it can be quite difficult to get the child incorporated into the desirable peer group, such that it can easily take *more* effort to get the student reintegrated and accepted back into the group than it would have been to address undesirable behaviors with different strategies. Effort that might have been used to teach math.

POINTS TO REMEMBER

- Don't ever use the power of the group against a student. If the group ostracizes someone, it might be difficult (or impossible) to reintegrate that student.
- Never alienate a child from being a recipient of your positive regard. The mental health costs to the student can be extreme and the social costs with peers can be irreparable.
- A group of students who know and adhere to your expectations will have a *huge* positive impact, while not alienating anyone. Plus, you have a whole group of potential peer tutors.
- Children can easily be taught that behaviors, like spelling words and math facts, can be learned by any member of the class, if they are expected, taught, and practiced.
- Ostracism from the peer group is associated with numerous negative outcomes—don't do it.

Readers who are interested in modeling and other effective behavioral strategies are encouraged to read one of the best references ever made available:

Alberto, P. A., & Troutman, A. C. (2006). *Applied behavior analysis for teachers* (7th Ed.). Columbus, Ohio: Pearson.

17

Moving Past Misbehavior

I went to see my best friend, whom I have known since junior high, a couple of months after his first son was born. Although I didn't understand the dynamics of his abrupt call asking for me to come visit him at the time, I learned later in my own life that he desperately *needed* me to visit, so that he would have an excuse to escape. The look of gratitude and relief evident on his face upon seeing me was heartwarming. He yelled over his shoulder to his wife that he was leaving, and, just as his right foot crossed the threshold of the kitchen door, just as freedom was within a few metatarsals of a break-neck run for sunshine and life, his wife yelled from the back of the house, "Change the baby before you go."

The look of paradise lost that immediately covered his face was frightening. He slowly turned, and we went back into the living room, where his son was in a playpen. How his wife knew a changing was needed I do not know. My friend leaned over, undid the diaper, and this man, who possessed a college degree and was pursuing a graduate degree, shouted "Goodgodamighty!" picked up his son, held him out, and said "you have to help me, I don't know how to do this."

I don't want to be indelicate, so I will simply say that the diaper, and a significant portion of the child, was covered with unpleasantness. That piece of information alone is enough for those of you with children to inspire shudders that traverse the length of your spinal cord with sufficient intensity to set off seismic monitors on the opposite side of the globe from where you sit.

I was in the kitchen, leaning on the island separating the kitchen and the living room, with a full view of the unfolding events. My friend was holding his child at arm's length, pointing the child toward the hallway. The child's mother came up the hallway saying, "Good grief, it's not rocket science; you just wipe him off and—"

As soon as her foot hit the living room, the child that was pointed at her began to tinkle with a force that I found surprising. This woman—my friend's wife—who also had a college degree and ran a very profitable business, at this point made a terrible mistake. Following the same logic, I assume, that leads the lone survivor in any scary movie to somehow get the upper hand on the villain and then, rather than retrieve some weapon that the now incapacitated villain had wielded and *instead run away unarmed*, this woman broke to her right instead of retreating back down the hall.

My friend never moved at all except, like the planet on which we live, for rotating on an invisible axis. His movement had the result of following his spouse as she circled around the living room while being chased by a stream of liquid that, from her reaction, you would guess contained some mixture of battery acid and the Ebola virus. The vile liquid was never farther than an inch from her heels as she ran around the room. On at least two laps, she actually attempted to go up onto the surface of the wall, *Matrix*-like, to escape. Crises like this distort perceptions, but the whole episode could not have lasted more than sixteen minutes. Surveying the scene afterward, I would estimate that this child had affected the living room of this ranch style home in roughly the same way as would an irrigation system affect a sod farm.

His wife then bade us leave. We scurried rodentlike from his home. We had a "boys' day out." We frolicked. We laughed and laughed about the incident that occurred right before we left his house. We laughed until, that is, the time began to draw near for him to return to the scene of the offending torrent. The closer we came to his curfew, the quieter he became. When we pulled into his driveway, he spoke not a word. We both walked slowly up the walk and entered his home.

The scene that greeted us was unbelievable. His wife was humming as she folded clothes. The baby was close by. She smiled at us, and asked if we'd had fun. My friend, who was expecting for the punishment to begin in earnest the minute he came home, was greeted in a welcoming way. His wife didn't even mention the household dousing, all signs of which *were gone*. The house even smelled sweetly of pine. Thinking she was putting on a show for me and would surely redress my friend in my absence, I called him later and asked what happened after I left. He said, "nothing." His wife had simply *moved on*. And eighteen years later, they are still married.

It's true that many new fathers will go to extreme measures to avoid diaper duty. They may ignore, flee, fib, and even act incompetent. But I don't think that was what my friend was doing. He was a new dad asked to do a task he didn't really want to complete, he was confronted with novel circumstances, and he was preoccupied with thinking about something else (leaving). Despite his being extremely intelligent, these factors, combined with his not having time to think about what to do, had an unfortunate and moist outcome. But that outcome didn't allow him to escape diaper duty for the rest of his days.

POINTS TO REMEMBER

- When undesirable behavior occurs, address it, but then *move on*.
- Do not bring up failures or problems from the past.

- Even the brightest student can perform below expectations when confronted with unknown expectations, situations, or circumstances, or when under stress.
- Do not allow poor performance to provide someone with an ongoing escape from an undesirable task.

The reader who knows someone who needs training on diaper duty and other baby things should refer that person to:

Kelly, M., & Parsons, E. (1975). *The mother's almanac.* New York: Doubleday.

Challenges for Children Today

Sometimes I think that I should make some money. I will be sitting in a quiet place, minding my own business, and this thought will simply happen *inside my own head.* I have even devised some ways to make some money. I'll tell you a great idea if you promise not to tell anybody. I read somewhere that you (and by you I mean somebody who has already made money) can purchase your very own personal submarine. By the way, I want my very own submarine very badly.

Here's the plan to make some money. I go and buy several lakefront lots. Then I buy a submarine. Then I get one of the big black straw-stuffed Halloween trash bags with scary orange eyes left over from terrorizing children who are frightened of straw-stuffed trash bags. By the way, I will use leftover bags as a *cost saver* to help keep my *bottom line* low (these are business terms I heard on an advertisement). Then I take the straw out of the trash bag, place it on the periscope of my personal submarine, and place my submarine in the lake upon whose shores I now own scads of lakefront property. I pilot my submerged submarine with the scary trash bag on the periscope of my submarine toward a large group of people on the shore of the lake. These people see the scary trash bag and think that there is some awful prehistoric creature evolved from cheap polyurethane living in the lake, and tell this to some person on television. The television person disseminates the report, and voilà—hoards of prehistoric polyurethane seekers want to see the "American Nessie with the Glowing Orange Eyes," so they offer me sums of money for my lakefront lots that are many multiples of what I originally paid. I sell the lakefront lots, but I *keep* my submarine.

When I attempted to implement my plan, I discovered a few minor problems. Perhaps the biggest problem is that, in order to get money to buy lakefront lots, the bank insisted that I would need something called "credit," which they assured me was "unlikely." The submarine people wouldn't even return my calls. But it's still interesting to me that I spontaneously think sometimes that I ought to make a wad of money. And I think that the thought has relevance to children being raised today.

Some researchers suggest that children now watch television for more hours a day than they are in school. This seems a tad unbalanced, since, considering the big picture, schools exist to propagate the knowledge that is deemed valuable and necessary to successful functioning in a civilized society, and television exists, as far as I can tell, solely to sell consumer goods (and not-so-goods) and services (and disservices). Therefore, I undoubtedly have spontaneous wealth fantasies in response to constant bombardment of televised insistence that I can acquire items that I can simply live without no longer, like a submarine. And I am weak-minded. However, since our national rate of personal income saving for 2006 was around *-1 percent*, I may not be the only one held sway by marketing power as seen on TV.

I think that there are more insidious effects that television is having on children. One issue worthy of our consideration is a phenomenon that I call the "victim star" (other people may use this or a similar term, but if so, I don't know about it), whereby those of us with no recognizable talent or abilities can still acquire our promised fifteen minutes of fame by going on television and letting other people treat us badly to amuse other people. We can let people treat us badly by diagnosing us, laughing at our singing, telling us we are ugly, throwing worms on us, firing us—there is a forum for just about any bad-treatment fetish. What chance does ten minutes per day of "character education" that children might receive in school have against six hours per day of uproarious, victimizing entertainment? Our culture apparently values celebrity above most other attributes, but society celebrates relatively few of us. Reality television places the ideal of celebrity within reach, if only fleetingly, by blessing us with the opportunity to be victim stars.

Considering that students benefit from the intellectual consumption of all of this televised frivolity *and* a smattering of schooling, it's hard to image how children, particularly boys, manage to fit so many hours per week into playing video games. Even though scores of studies speak of the negative mental health impact associated with high rates of video gaming (particularly observed increases in aggression), this cloud has a silver lining. A recent study suggests that the time children spend scanning the televised nether worlds for things that need a killing is very helpful at helping them become good with visual scanning activities like finding your lost car keys.

Access to stimulation is everywhere, so it's not surprising that students today expect to be constantly stimulated. This expectation was communicated by a good friend of mine recently. He is a teacher, and his class and several others, all middle schoolers, had boarded buses and were soon bound for a field trip. Another teacher stepped onto the bus my friend was on and announced that the caravan would be pulling out in five minutes. A middle school girl sitting in front of my friend reached in her purse, pulled out a cell phone, called a friend, and said, "God, I'm bored." It's striking that we have lost the ability to be without active stimulation for five minutes. I believe that we lost this ability in the late 1970s, when disco officially died.

The list of challenges faced by youth today is nearly endless. What difference can you make? The first thing that you can do is show students an alternative, rather than telling them that they should live differently. If you tell them not to ridicule other students, not to bully, not to laugh at others in pain, but then you giggle with a teacher in the hallway about the pathetic performance and the hilarious, brutal feedback directed at some buffoon on a hit television show, you have liberally sprinkled powdered sugar on the forbidden brownie. The temptation for many kids to take a furtive lick is increased, not decreased.

Another thing that you can do is *teach* (bit of a recurring theme, huh?). If you think empathy for others is important, teach empathy for others with a level of *intensity, sincerity, and frequency* that actually competes with opposite lessons being taught in high definition (where available). If you think that there are other indices of the value of a life besides the number of toys accumulated along the way, don't scratch off lottery tickets during intercom announcements. If you think patience and quiet reflection have value, teach and model these skills in a way that is meaningful and developmentally appropriate.

There is one final step that you can take. If you have thought carefully about something to which your children or students can gain easy access, and if you have decided that access is harmful for students, it may be something that is worth your making a professional statement by removing your financial support. If it's a television show, you can withdraw your support by not watching it—or not buying products that sponsor the show. If it's a product—say, a product containing alcohol—that has a marketing approach that demeans or exploits women, don't buy it.

Before undertaking these strategies, though, consider two points. First, if you have thoughtfully considered the evidence and decided that you cannot support something because of the potential detriment to youth, *start your campaign with something you like a great deal.* There is little substance in withdrawing your support from a product you never purchase, and the risk is significant that such efforts will be seen by students as empty moralizing based on trying to sell everyone on your philosophy. If you have decided that a television show teaches lessons and values that are contrary to those lessons and values that you value and teach, and if you *really love that show,* this is a good starting place for making a sacrifice.

Second, if you have decided that your professional integrity will no longer accommodate sustaining your support of a product, show, and so on, and you have decided on withdrawing your support, be prepared to have some of that patience that we were talking about your teaching to your students a couple of paragraphs ago. It's unlikely that your changing the channel, even when augmented by your passionate telephone calls to a television station, will generate immediate results. My having said that, numerous examples indicate slow change has been the observed result of the commitments of certain resolute people who decided to make a stand concerning an issue they thought valuable. The increasing availability of organic food products in mainline grocery stores is one example of this phenomenon. If you do decide that such a commitment is one that you can and should support—say you no longer, for example, can support a television show by no longer viewing it—there is one other important benefit. You could spend the time you had previously spent watching mindless drivel working on a strict personal budget. It may be a pipe dream, but let's shoot for getting that savings rate up to 0 percent next year—they aren't giving away those submarines.

POINTS TO REMEMBER

- If there are traits and behaviors that you value in children, model them. One display of hypocrisy between what you do and what you say can undo dozens of previous positive examples and hundreds of verbalizations.

- If traits and behaviors are important, they must be taught. The character traits that we value most, like empathy and patience, develop throughout the life span if taught and nurtured.
- You can make a professional and personal statement that impacts the "big picture" by withdrawing your support from things that you know can harm your students. If you decide to make this commitment, start with withdrawing your support for something that you will really miss.

The reader who has misplaced his or her car keys may want to read:

Dingfelder, S. E. (2007). Your brain on video games. *Monitor on Psychology.* Retrieved October 2, 2007, from http://www.apa.org/monitor/feb07/yourbrain.html

The readers interested in how much money they are not saving can see:

Bureau of Economic Analysis. (2006). *Personal income and outlays: June 2006 revised estimates.* News release. Washington, DC: United States Department of Commerce. Retrieved October 2, 2007, from http://www.bea.gov/bea/newsrelarchive/2006/pi0606.pdf

Or they could just review their credit card statement.

19
Using Finesse

In reading, on television, or in conversation with another person, you may at some point have heard that a task was like trying to "catch a greased pig." This simile is intended to convey the idea that a task is difficult. Unfortunately, the simile is a bit misleading. If you are fleet of foot (and, of course, if you have the desire), you can *catch* a greased pig. *Holding* a greased pig is an entirely different issue. I know this because a boy with whom I went to school released a greased pig at his high school graduation ceremony. This pig proved quite difficult for numerous highly trained educators to hold, even though it was caught several times. It may not surprise you to know that this boy was a good bit older than his fellow graduates, nor that he was a friend of mine.

His family farmed, and he had numerous responsibilities. One day he was trying to pry a stump out of the ground with a large metal pry bar. The bar slipped off of the root of the stump and hit his left arm quite hard. He was surprised that he felt no pain. Curious, he used his right arm to again strike his left arm with the large metal bar. This time his curiosity was satisfied when he experienced acute pain resulting from a broken left arm. Later on, as an adult, he woke to the alarm clock one morning. He got out of bed and started the bath water, after which he returned to bed. He awoke sometime later to the sound of running water, to the sight of a flooded house, and to the vision of a clock that proclaimed that he was significantly tardy from his job. He went to his safe and retrieved a .44 magnum. Clint Eastwood fans may recall his character Dirty Harry referring to this particular caliber as the "most powerful handgun in the world." My friend used this device to shoot holes in the floor of his home, so that the water would drain out. As a point of interest, my pinky finger fits easily into the hole made by his .44 magnum.

You may be picturing the life of this person as a bit full-steam-ahead-ish. He is the proverbial bull in a china shop (and armed to the teeth, to boot). You may have known people like this, and have undoubtedly seen how they interact with other people. You may even be related to some of these people, probably by marriage. These kind of people frequently attempt to bulldog others into conforming to their views. Any behavior that inspires their disapproval is met with immediate confrontation and correction. These people make good prison guards and often find work in service industries. While there is an argument to be made for providing immediate feedback and clear expectations (in fact, the arguments were made *very effectively* in previous chapters of this book), there is also something to be said for having a soft touch, what I call using finesse.

One of the things that keep me interested in working with people is that people are peculiar. This characteristic of peculiarity fascinates me, but it drives some people straight up the wall and into the banking profession. Far too frequently, people do *exactly the opposite* of what we would assume that they should do. A good example of this from a mental health perspective is *cognitive dissonance.* Many of you may be familiar with the concept proposed by Leon Festinger, which in the broadest sense refers to a kind of psychological equilibrium that we strive to maintain; that inconsistent thoughts and beliefs are unpleasant, and we try to achieve psychic consistency. Hundreds (if not thousands) of studies support the concept, which has a few main tenets. I will focus on one—referred to as the *minimal justification hypothesis.*

In one avenue of his research, Festinger did a famous experiment sometimes called the $1/$20 experiment. Simply stated, what Festinger did was take groups of people and make each person in each group do an extremely boring task. Afterward, they were each supposed to tell another person how wonderfully exciting the boring task was—that is, to lie. He paid the people in one group $1 to tell this lie, and paid the people in the other group $20 (not a bad piece of change when the experiment was done in the 1950s) to tell the lie. After all of this was done, Festinger asked the people in each group how much they had enjoyed doing the boring task. Intuitively, you would probably guess that the people who had been paid $20 rated the task as more enjoyable—but you would be wrong. The people who were paid $1 *raved* about the boring task, likening it to a trip to Happyville to ride the roller coaster and eat cotton candy.

The explanation for this is that the dissonance created by lying to another person for only $1 was too unpleasant for most people to live with. Therefore, to create consonance, the people in the $1 group convinced themselves that they really enjoyed the boring task. Before you pooh-pooh too much, consider this. A confusing thing occurred during the Korean War. Some of our prisoners of war began renouncing the United States and joined the Communist Party. No, they weren't tortured into converting. The way to make captured soldiers renounce some of their strongest beliefs was to entice them with small rewards like cigarettes to do small things, like take better food than other prisoners. The cognitive dissonance caused by selling ideals for trinkets was so discomforting that some changed their beliefs to match their behaviors.

What difference does any of this make? Festinger's (and subsequently others') work suggests that getting people to do what we want them to do (like participate in school) with tweaks and nudges may be much better at getting others to buy into something they don't want to do (like participate in school) than big ticket bribes and threats. Put another way, Festinger's work could suggest that those who attempt behavior change with a soft approach and finesse could be more successful than those bulldog, bull-in-the-china-shop people who tend to use force and grand gestures. Sometimes a mop just works better than a magnum.

> ## Points to Remember
>
> - You have more control of your classroom by letting students have some personal control and choice of what occurs in the classroom.
> - If a child does not like school, sometimes the smallest behavioral compliance that you can manufacture can begin to snowball into additional successes that put a student on a trajectory leading toward school achievement.
> - Festinger's work is important because it provides good evidence that forming attitudes is not always a prerequisite to getting desired behavior. If you can finesse the preferred behaviors into occurring, preferred attitudes sometimes follow.

The reader who is interested in some of the classic work on cognitive dissonance should check out:

Festinger, L., & Carlsmith, J. M. (1959). Cognitive consequences of forced compliance. *Journal of Abnormal and Social Psychology, 58*, 203–210.

20

The Inevitable Attack

From the time that I was old enough to notice such things and right up to this very day, my dad has demonstrated an eccentricity. In every vehicle that he has ever owned, from the time the vehicle was driven into our yard until it passed to another owner, my dad had a piece of dental floss draped across the gear shifter. This is the type of factoid that a person desperately wishes was made up; unfortunately in this case it's not. I have never seen him use it for anything. The floss is simply there, just as floss has been since he drove vehicles that looked as if they had been constructed from lawn mower parts as a second grade art project right up through his current (retired) preference for luxury vehicles. Luxury vehicles adorned with dental hygiene equipment. Incidentally, I noticed that his taste in automobiles changed in proportion to the number of teenaged boys who were no longer available to drive them.

Over the years, I developed numerous theories to explain the presence of the floss. I hypothesized that it was there, like tying a string around his finger, to remind him of something. I hypothesized that it was heirloom floss, inherited from a special relative and having special significance. I hypothesized that he was actually a CIA assassin whose weapon of choice was dental floss—a master of the silent art who left no clues except unexplained wax residue and a minty smell around the necks of enemies of the state.

Having become a highly trained mental health professional (probably because of eccentricities like the floss thing), I have changed my opinions. I think that behavior occurs because it serves a useful (practical) function. I think that the simplest hypothesis is often the best hypothesis. I have to admit to myself that my dad's floss does not serve a romantic, deadly purpose. I think he keeps it there so that, if tooling in retired bliss down the interstate and stricken suddenly with the realization that two or more teeth are troubled by the presence of an annoying particle of food, he can immediately rid himself of the offending material. Not romantic at all, but maybe a bit gross. And considering his mental state, are those of us traveling the same highways in other vehicles safer when his car is moving down the road and both of his hands are engaged in dental hygiene or when his hands are on the steering wheel?

An unfortunate eventuality that we who are teacher educators have inadequately addressed is the knowledge that children may strike out at you. Even if you have every child's best interests at heart and teach with sincerity and passion. You may work extra hours and attend all school-related functions. Regardless, there is a good chance that, at some point, you will be attacked by a student. This attack may not be physical—in fact, it probably won't be. It may be that a child lashes out at you verbally. It may be that you put your heart into trying to reach an ostracized child who seemingly remains unresponsive to all of your efforts. Whether the attack takes the form of rejection, verbal attacks, accusations, or a child does become physical, these rejections are hurtful to any adult who cares about their students.

You might remember what happened to Roy Horn, of Siegfried and Roy fame, a few years ago. During their famous act at Las Vegas—featuring trained tigers that lived with the entertainers—Roy was attacked by one of those tigers. He suffered injuries that resulted in his leaving show business. Although an official investigation by the U.S. Department of Agriculture failed to identify a cause for the attack, Roy maintains that the tiger was trying to help him after he fainted on stage as a result of high blood pressure. Roy has adamantly maintained that the tiger shouldn't be killed because of the bite.

If you rely heavily on punishment, if you clearly prefer some students over others, if you're coercive in your attempts to have your expectations met, if you use embarrassment as a method of behavior management, if you give more negative feedback than positive feedback, if you allow any students to fail at a high rate, and if under these circumstances a student lashes out at you, you are at the very least partially to blame. On the other hand, if you base your approach to child behavior management on the ideas presented in this book, you will be increasing the odds that children will behave in the ways that you desire and that they will experience school success. If your efforts systematically focus on including all students, programming for success, finding things to like in all children, trying to teach through inspiring the interests and curiosity of students, and if under these circumstances a student lashes out at you, it's much less likely that you share the blame. Under these circumstances, a child who lashes out is like dental floss on the gear shifter. No clear explanation may be obvious, but at least you didn't put the floss on the gear shifter.

It's important to consider that many factors can contribute to a child's lashing out. Some of the factors that may be associated with such lashing out include anxiety or fear, some form of *diathesis* like prenatal problems or neurological insult, a learned response to perceived threat, or a misunderstanding or misinterpretation of your thoughts, actions, or words. Some children become aggressive because of harsh treatment or abuse they experienced elsewhere. Some children act out because they may feel safe enough to act out at school, while their behavior is highly structured—perhaps tightly controlled and rigidly enforced—in other settings. Some children grow up in neighborhoods that can best be described as war zones, in which violence, crime, and exploitation are daily observances. Some children lash out as a result of real or perceived bullying, teasing, or the ongoing exclusion from peer relationships. Some children simply lash out because aggression is very effective in getting them what they want—at least in the short term.

Based on hundreds of conversations with teachers, I feel confident that responding in a constructive way to a student who has attacked us—through words, physical attempts to intimidate, threats, or physical confrontation—is the most challenging professional hurdle that many teachers ever face. Many teachers had never considered the real possibility that a student would lash out at them. When teachers respond to these episodes with aggression or avoidance, or by demanding an overwhelming punitive response, the results that people have related to me have been tremendously detrimental for everyone involved. Some teachers have become almost paralyzed, losing the ability to effectively teach. Some have seen their relationships with *all* students deteriorate. Some have left the field.

I'm not suggesting that you not impose consequences if a student attacks you in some way. I only encourage you to consider the larger picture and the long-term outcome you desire. I encourage you to consider the goal of the school in which you work. I hope that you consider the educational impact of your response. You should impose reasonable consequences— and then you should move on. Part of the moving on process involves learning to listen very, very carefully. I have found that, if we listen very carefully, a student will usually communicate her needs clearly. Students may communicate their needs behaviorally rather than orally, but they will communicate.

Teachers have more of an impact on children than any other professional group. The impact that we have is often entwined with hard choices that we have to make—often about students with whom we struggle. All of your students will learn important lessons from your response to difficult situations. As a result of challenges in the classroom, just like my dad, when you retire from education, you will have earned the right to be a little peculiar, with or without dental floss.

POINTS TO REMEMBER

- If you haven't been told before, I'm telling you now—you will, if you teach long enough, become the target of a child's aggression. This aggression may be physical, but is much more likely to be verbal or manifest as rejection.
- Whatever form aggression toward you takes, it is painful.
- Keep in mind, and this statement isn't overly dramatic, that your reaction to difficult situations can affect a student's entire school career.
- Other students in the classroom will learn more by your handling of difficult situations than your handling of routine situations.

Readers interested in the tiger attack on Roy Horn can see an overview at:

http://www.imdb.com/title/tt0182299/news

21

Calling for Help

$\mathbf{B}$ esides being a college professor, I do consultation in schools. If a student has challenging behavior that hasn't responded to things that have been tried by school personnel, sometimes an administrator will call me and ask something like, "Can you come and fix this?" I will inevitably say something like, "Beats me, but we can give it a try." It seems to me that as a society we have developed and promoted the idea that, if I relate my personal story to an "expert" for three to five minutes, the expert can then give us not only a diagnosis, but the formula for solving all of our problems as well. By some standards, I could be considered an expert in the area of child mental health, and I have never felt like I could solve anything—let alone try to understand another person—in three to five minutes.

Despite teachers' being surrounded by people during the entire school day, teaching is an isolated vocation. Teachers have little opportunity to interact with other adults throughout the workday. There is *no amount of training* that we could provide in college that would sufficiently prepare people for the diversity and complexity of needs and behaviors that you will see when you actually enter the classroom. Yet there is often little support once you get in your classroom and close the door. You will be observed by administrators, but these observations are often for evaluation purposes, not for the purpose of assistance and support. Some teachers make the reasonable assumption that seeking help from building administrators will be perceived as a lack of professional competence. It's easy to form the same impression if an "expert" is called in to help with a student in your classroom.

I can't speak for all "experts," but I can assure you that I do not enter anyone's classroom assuming that the teacher is incompetent. Additionally, I would *never* insult a teacher by pretending that I have conjured the answer to a behavioral challenge in three to five minutes. And last, anybody that offers his or her help by telling you what you *should have done* needs to be subjected to a behavior management plan based primarily on punishment. It's easy to say what someone else should have done when you weren't around.

Everyone who works with students will be challenged at some point by a particularly taxing behavior. Even though it may become deathly quiet when an administrator enters your classroom, that quiet would likely disappear quickly if the administrator was in there every day. After a while the novelty will wear off, even for the principal. This leads to a cardinal rule of working with children that you must memorize immediately: It's not okay to ask for help—*it's absolutely essential.*

If you're in a teacher preparation program, start thinking right now about the support system that you might develop when you get your first teaching position. I don't know how I would have managed my first year of teaching if it hadn't been for a very talented and experienced paraprofessional who was also in the classroom. I quickly found teachers to be the most generous, willing professionals on the planet to share ideas and offer assistance. When I taught at other schools (even after I had "experience"), I always sought out and easily found a mentor teacher to help me get oriented and moving in the right direction. Though they may seem intimidating, good administrators can provide a world of assistance—and often actually provide it. If you're hesitant about approaching administrators for help, there are numerous other professionals that should be available to help you, including school counselors, school psychologists, and school social workers. *You* are the one who is at the school to provide direct service to children. It's the job of everybody else on the payroll to provide whatever you need to make sure that the job gets done well.

And don't forget about your professors—I get calls all the time from previous teacher candidates who ask my opinion about a behavioral issue. And it isn't unusual for me to call one of my previous students who is now teaching school to ask her opinion about a behavioral issue.

It isn't possible, nor is it reasonable, to think that you—or anybody—can or will have all of the answers about how best to work with every child. As previously mentioned, I believe teachers to be the most giving professionals of any field. I have found them to be available and willing to help out in any way—from lending an ear to offering an opinion to sharing materials. The Internet is absolutely replete with materials that have been posted by teachers—from lesson plans to behavior plans to Web quests—posted for the sole purpose of sharing ideas with colleagues. You don't see many stockbrokers doing that.

There is value in what you have chosen to do professionally, and many, many people are grateful that you have chosen to do it. The administrative infrastructure of a school system exists to help you do your job, so don't be afraid to ask. Your colleagues, who are doing the same job that you do every day, are a vast resource. Books, journals, and conferences are excellent sources of information. The amount of material posted on the Internet for teachers, by teachers, is amazing. Even though teaching can seem an isolated job, you are never alone.

Points to Remember

- Most of us are mindful of the immense value of the job that you do—and we need to be more vocal with our gratitude.
- Even though you might feel isolated in your classroom, your colleagues are generous, understanding, and available to you if you need help.
- Though they may seem intimidating to ask, administrators are there as resources, not as roadblocks, to effectively working with students.
- You can find tons of materials on the Internet—but be a discriminating shopper.
- Don't neglect professional reading. Set a goal and read some number of professional books each year. Find one journal in your teaching area and subscribe to it. There is no substitute if you really want to stay current.

22

Conclusion

Every Therapy Has a Success Story

The mandates of the federal law known as No Child Left Behind have forced those of us involved in teacher preparation to emphasize that people who are in—or who are entering—the teaching field must be "highly qualified." This translates into, among other things, an increased focus on ensuring that anyone who teaches children must have significant training in the content (whether math, science, or English) that they teach. It's hard to argue against the need to know the material that you teach to children.

However, teacher training was already a full college curriculum before this law was mandated, so the question for those of us who teach teachers was: "What do we teach *less of* to meet the requirement of what has to be taught *more of?*" One piece of feedback that I hear repeatedly from school administrators is that new entrants to the field know the content, but they can't teach it as effectively as they otherwise might because of behavior problems in the classroom. I have heard this same concern expressed by Sunday school teachers, Cub Scout leaders, parents—anyone involved in the lives of today's youth. Often, this thought is followed by a statement that—if not a verbatim comment, strongly resembles—"kids today are different. The things that I used to do don't seem to help."

I think that we should acknowledge that (as anyone who has taught for several years will attest) kids today are different. Consider some of the differences facing a child growing up today compared to a child growing up ten to fifteen years ago. The environment has changed. The curriculum standards and expectations in schools have changed. The economy has changed. Entertainment options have changed. Pressures on parents have changed. Some of these changes are good, but some are bad—and unfortunately, some are both. For example, one description that I hear used to characterize today's youth is "sophisticated." Sure, children are sophisticated because they have access to an incomprehensible volume of information that is growing at an exponential rate—and knowledge is good. Of course, children also might access information that they are developmentally not prepared to handle—the opposite, less glamorous side of sophistication. I would agree that children today are different, but different doesn't mean "worse." It means "not the same."

I also agree that, for a variety of reasons, the things that were done commonly in classrooms twenty years ago may be insufficient to address the behavioral needs of many students today. It probably won't help to identify specific children as being "worse" than other children. I am told, at least on a weekly basis by people who interact with kids, something like, "I don't have any trouble with most of my kids—but those three (or two, or twelve) just don't get it."

What may be helpful in situations like this is for us to change our approach. Using school as an example, it may well be true that the behavior management strategies that are used in a classroom work for many kids. These strategies may have worked with previous kids in previous classrooms. But that doesn't necessarily mean that there was a great, world-class behavior management plan in place. It may mean that a lot of kids do okay with prompts, warnings, and a progression of consequences—the types of plans that are most common in schools. In my experience, though, the minute you put one or two kids who do have more pronounced needs in a group behavior, often the behavior of the whole group, becomes a real problem.

Several years ago, I found myself in the position of being away from home a good deal of the time. Thinking that my absences must have been nearly intolerable, I decided to surprise my wife with the gift of a puppy to help ease the desperate loneliness that she must have felt. I picked a female white German shepherd. What a great choice. My wife was pleased; she even managed to play-act convincingly that my work jaunts were hardly noticed, and we named the puppy Snowflake.

Snowflake grew quickly, bonded with us completely, and, as an added bonus, was protective. I only taught her one or two tricks. She didn't need any behavior management. She housebroke herself. She even wiped her paws when she came in the house. If I wanted Snowflake to do something, I would look her in the eye and tell her. She would thoughtfully consider what I said, nod slightly, and do what I asked. Sometimes I could tell that she thought that my idea was really dumb, and she would look at me patiently, as if I was a babbling chimpanzee, but then she would placate me by complying—if she really wanted to.

As Snowflake aged, she began to develop health problems. Despite ongoing veterinary care, we were told that Snowflake's health would get progressively worse—quickly. Grieving, but especially concerned about our daughters, both of whom had known Snowflake their entire lives, my wife and I decided to get another dog. We knew that Snowflake could never be replaced, but we were a pet family, and we thought that a new playmate would be good for everybody.

We went to the pound to see if there was a dog that we could rescue and who would also be a good fit with our family. Especially sensitive to our impending loss, we wanted to save a life if we could. We saw a mixed breed hound dog leaning against a cage as we walked past. She was already grown, somewhere between one and two years old. We stroked her and she looked at us. The people at the pound said that her odds of adoption were low—everybody preferred puppies. We went back and looked again. She was quiet and gentle. I could tell just from looking in her eyes that she had attained the pinnacle of Maslow's hierarchy of needs. Her cage was clean. We had found our dog.

We took our new dog home. Snowflake seemed thrilled. After a little discussion, we decided to name the new member of the family Bumpus. You may remember meeting Bumpus in a previous chapter, or you might recognize the name from one of my favorite movies—*A Christmas Story*. The movie is about a little boy named Ralphie who has one burning desire—to get a Red Ryder BB gun for Christmas. Next door to Ralphie lived a family that owned a slew of dirty, smelly hound dogs. Their last name was Bumpus. Bumpus spent the weekend quietly following us around—learning the rules, I assumed. The day was Saturday.

On Monday, we made an appointment to see our vet. A rule of pet adoption was that you must schedule your adopted pet for spaying or neutering and for a thorough physical examination. The appointment was made, and on the specified day, we took Bumpus to see the vet. We thought that we would be dropping her off to be spayed, but the vet dutifully examined her first. After doing some tests, the vet explained that there would be no surgery on that day. Bumpus was sick, with a potentially dangerous infection commonly associated with boarding (or dog pound) conditions. Get Bumpus well, we were told, then surgery. The vet gave us medicine and said that Bumpus would start to feel better in a couple of days. The day was Thursday.

On Saturday, we woke up to what sounded like a buzz saw. Bumpus, in a manner made popular by the tornado in *The Wizard of Oz*, was spinning around the laundry room in which she had been allowed to sleep, spreading debris like confetti. The room, unlike her cage at the pound, wasn't clean. Evidence that she was not housebroken was provided to my brain by three of the five human senses. I let her into the yard. Looking out, I saw that Bumpus was running in circles with such enthusiasm that she was kicking up divots with every step. In the distance, a train whistle sounded. Bumpus stopped running, gazed off in the distance, and howled a response. When the train whistle quieted, Bumpus started running again. And so the weekend went. It began to dawn on us that, frankly, Bumpus had issues.

For those of us who try to separate "what works" from "what does not work," one question we are addressing is cause and effect. Put another way, did my intervention (behavior management strategy) *cause* the observed behavior change (Bumpus limited toileting to the great outdoors)? A common happenstance is that people will observe something that occurs with the effect, and assume that there is a causal relationship when in fact they observed a coincidence that occurred with (or prior to) the effect. For example, some observant social scientists once noted that, as ice cream consumption within a geographic location increased, the crime rate increased as well. Thus, eating ice cream causes us to break the law—or not. This phenomenon is a *correlation*. Two things occur together, so you might conclude that a relationship exists, but not necessarily a causal (or in any way a meaningful) relationship. If you think about it, there are other factors more likely to be meaningfully related to the crime rate, like the weather. Even criminals like warm feet.

Another phenomenon that leads us to sometimes think that one thing caused another is the placebo effect. A placebo is anything that we do that doesn't really help more than doing nothing at all. If you are testing a new medicine, you give a placebo to one group and the actual medicine to another group. In order for you to think that the medicine works, it should not just help, it should have *more* of an impact than the placebo. This gets complicated, because some people with medical conditions will improve after getting a placebo, and some people getting a placebo will *develop negative side effects,* even if they only took a sugar pill. Having negative results from a "nontreatment," much less frequently discussed than the placebo effect (which involves positive effects resulting from a nontreatment), is called the *nocebo effect.* It gets even more complicated when talking about behavior or mental health, because the placebo effect can be different, depending on the problem. For example, as many as 70 percent of people suffering from excessive anxiety will respond favorably to a placebo.

This leads to an important observation about behavior. Virtually every therapy or intervention has a success story. That doesn't mean that every therapy works equally well, and some interventions even make things systematically worse. But it's almost certain that somewhere, somebody will say, "All you need to get rid of that wart is some stump water, then you cipher this chant. It worked for my cousin." A spin of that saying might be, "I didn't have to do that for my other [insert preferred term—dog, child, students, whatever]." Maybe what was done before had a placebo effect. Maybe it worked great for kids with minimal behavior support needs. Maybe kids today are different. Different dogs have different needs. Different kids have different needs. And maybe it doesn't even matter what explanation we come up with. If you are like most of the people that I know who work with children, what really matters to you is that there are kids who have unmet needs, and the good news is that there are things that we can do to really increase the odds of improving their quality of life—beginning with their behavior.

I have to be honest. "To thine own self be true," exhorted Shakespeare, which, where I grew up, would be translated to read, "to my own self be true." Snowflake's behavior and rapidity of becoming housebroken was not evidence that I am a dog whisperer—which I learned when I met Bumpus. Snowflake didn't need behavior support, and I met her level of need in the area of behavior support (which was *none*) by providing the needed behavior support (none). And I could use the same strategies (none) with Bumpus that had worked so well with Snowflake, and they would not have been sufficient to effect a desired behavior change. They probably would have been sufficient to cause a lot of stress to both of us. I'm fairly sure that I was speaking to Bumpus in canine, but she must have been listening in feline.

Bumpus was amenable to behavior change, however, just like we all are. We had to consciously and systematically use some targeted behavior strategies—like the ones discussed in this book—to help Bumpus become successfully incorporated into our (potty trained) pack. We didn't use punishment or shout or stomp our feet, all of which could have made things worse. We matched her level of need (some), with the level of intervention provided (some). She will *never* be a Snowflake, and we will never ask her to be. But she sure is comforting, with her head on my leg and her big hound eyes looking sympathetic and self-actualized. She's not "worse" than Snowflake, she's different, and she offers us different things and she has different needs. And that is just fine.

POINTS TO REMEMBER

- You can expect to get lots of advice when you start your teaching career—some solicited and some unsolicited.
- The value of advice is much like the value of jewelry. It depends on the quality and workmanship that went into an individual piece, and the quality is sometimes hard to judge at first glance.
- There will be people who insist that, if you want to effectively deal with classroom behavioral issues, you use strategies that are at odds with the principles discussed in this book. Before you follow *any* advice:
  o Do some research. You don't have to take my word for anything.
  o Think about how *you* want to be treated.
  o Think about how you would want *your children* treated.
- Now go and enjoy the challenges, thrills, doubts, and victories associated with doing the most important job in history—teaching children.

For additional reading about correlations, the interested reader can see further detail related to the example of ice cream and crime and determining cause and effect in:

Salkind, N. J. (2003). *Statistics for people who think they hate statistics.* Thousand Oaks, CA: Sage.

For additional reading about the placebo effect and her evil and less popular twin the nocebo effect, interesting discussion can be found in:

Roberts, R., & Groome, D. (2001). *Parapsychology: The science of unusual experience.* New York: Edward Arnold.

For additional reading about anxiety, including a good discussion of intervention options (including the placebo effect), see:

Mellinger, D., & Lynn, S. J. (2003). *The monster in the cave: How to face your fear and anxiety and live your life.* New York: Berkley.

For further reading on alternative therapies for warts, see:

Twain, M. (1903). *The adventures of Mark Twain.* New York: Harper and Brothers.

Index

CORWIN
PRESS

The Corwin Press logo—a raven striding across an open book—represents
the union of courage and learning. Corwin Press is committed to improving
education for all learners by publishing books and other professional
development resources for those serving the field of PreK–12 education. By
providing practical, hands-on materials, Corwin Press continues to carry out
the promise of its motto: **"Helping Educators Do Their Work Better."**